A PRESENCE OF THE LIVING GOD THROUGH HIS SELF-REVEALED NAMES

DOW F. ROBINSON

gabriella
PRESS

Cultivating the Presence of the Living God through His Self-Revealed Names

Copyright © 2013, 2014 The estate of Dow F. Robinson
All rights reserved

Second edition, October 2014

ISBN-13: 978-1502515452
ISBN-10: 1502515458

Gabriella Press: www.gabriellapress.com
Bulk order pricing is available.

Editor: Dorothy Leal
Cover: Steve Tyrrell / www.tyrrellcreative.com
Production: Bill Leal

Unless otherwise noted, Scripture is taken from the HOLY BIBLE, NEW INTERNATIONAL VERSION®. Copyright © 1973, 1978, 1984 International Bible Society. Used by permission of Zondervan. All rights reserved.

Contents

Introduction 1

Section One. Worshiping YHWH in the Adamic Era 12

    1. Elohim, the One Who Begins Everything 15

    2. YHWH Elohim, the Powerful and Relational One Who Self-Exists 27

Section Two. Worshiping YHWH in the Abrahamic Era 37

    3. El Elyon, God Most High 43

    4. Adonai, Sovereign One 51

    5. El Shaddai, God Almighty 59

Section Three. Worshiping YHWH in the Mosaic Era 67

    6. The Great I AM 71

    7. The LORD 80

Section Four. Worshiping YHWH in the Prophetic Era 91

    8. Qadosh, the One Who Is Holy 98

    9. Qabod, the Glory of Israel 108

Section Five. Worshiping YHWH in the New Testament Era 119

    10. Jesus and Father 125

    11. God and Father of Our Lord Jesus Christ 136

Section Six. Worshiping YHWH in the Present Age and Age to Come 145

    12. Worshiping YHWH through Jesus in the Holy Spirit 149

    13. Worshiping YHWH, the One-Who-Sits-On-The-Throne 162

    14. Worshiping YHWH, the Lion-Lamb 168

Appendices 177

    Summary of God's Self-Revealed Names 179

    YHWH in David's Psalms 183

    Worship Words 201

    Recommendations for Further Study 203

Editor's Note

The original draft of this book was written by Dow over the last years of his life. I worked with him extensively in the year before his Homegoing to produce this text—what a privilege. This second edition includes many corrections and some restructuring of material to highlight Dow's heart and voice. It was a privilege to work with Dow and touch the very Presence of God as he shared his wisdom and passion for relational worship of YHWH Elohim.

I'm also deeply grateful for the help of my husband Bill, with handling the whole publishing process, and for his personal support of both Dow and I during the lengthy process of writing and editing.

Steve Tyrell once again gave generously of his time to guide the revised design of the whole book, as well as to produce a cover that so strikingly expresses the Presence of YHWH. May Father reward him many times over.

May this work from Dow's heart bless you with his Presence as much as it has blessed those of us who have helped bring it to birth.

> Dorothy Leal
> Columbus, Ohio
> October, 2014

Preface

What is so critical to our relationship with God that we need yet another book on the names of God? There are two reasons. First, we need to know what names God himself most closely associated with his Person and Presence. These are the names that God chose to reveal, not the names that his followers or others have called him over the ages. So while there are many names of Father, Son and Spirit found in Scripture, this book examines the ones YHWH himself selected.

Second, we need to know how God revealed his names to his people over the millennia so that we can learn how we also can draw into his Presence in a filial relationship through these specific names; that is, relational worship. The goal of personal salvation is worship. However, we as Christians often find ourselves consumed by focusing all of life around ourselves. This postmodern depletion of our existence develops into a sickness among believers today, a spirit-sickness characterized by a lack of relational worship with the living God, missing the life-giving presence of YHWH Elohim.

> **The Spirit's eternal love song among the triune God spills over into earth's populations through his self-revealed names**

Inevitably, we come to sense a craving in our inner self that nothing can satisfy. Our Christianity becomes anemic, almost pointless. For God created us in such a way that we have within ourselves an area specially modeled for his presence and for interaction with him. This mute yet irrepressible yearning defies all attempts at satisfaction without an interactive, relational worship of Father, incarnate in Jesus Christ, Son of the Living God.

The Spirit's cry for worship arises to destroy the feeble and suffocating substitutes for God-worship. The Spirit's eternal love song among the triune God spills over into earth's populations, stirs that empty area in all of us, sets us hungering and thirsting again for the One whose life-giving water quenches every thirst. When worship of God does not result in fellowship with God, then let it be blown away like chaff before the Spirit's wind. Let it be purged like dross from the refiner's fire. Then let real worship begin!

YHWH ELOHIM

Sourced in Scriptures,
    written by mortal men,
        that we might come to know relationally
            the One who is YHWH Elohim.
A gradual and measured release through the centuries
    about himself, who is YHWH Elohim.
        To each age, God released more details about himself,
            and at any one point in time, the self-revelation is entirely accurate yet partial and incomplete.
The fullness, the full edition, of YHWH'S self-revelation
    we find only in Jesus of Nazareth, crowned Jesus Christ, at Father's right hand.
        An open display, through intrusive acts in human history, of the unimaginable dimensions in YHWH Elohim's identity.
        Through mere humans like Enoch, Noah, Abraham, Hagar, Isaac, David, Isaiah, Paul, John…. and you.
A self-portrait or depiction, by self-revelatory events,
    of the exquisite details inherent in the nature of
        YHWH Elohim.
YHWH Elohim,
    who is Father-Son-Spirit,
        opens himself to Scripture-writers
            whose message draws people
                as worshipers of YHWH Elohim.

Introduction

God's Initiation of Relationship

Worship is the practice of our relationship with YHWH Elohim, the God and Father of our Lord Jesus Christ. What Father wants above all else is that we learn how to practice a yielded relationship with him, paid for in the blood of Jesus of Nazareth.

> **Worship is the practice of our relationship with YHWH Elohim, the God and Father of our Lord Jesus Christ**

Mere physical posture or memorized prayers are often little more than self-exalting outlays of energy, time, and resources. While these may look good on the outside, they guarantee a suffocating and enervating blight on our worship-relationship with Father. Father looks for a faith-attitude, a bright and vigorous searching for himself, an impassioned, pestering and dogged—even violent—chase after himself. For in that same way he longs to connect with us: vigorously, intimately, longingly.

WORSHIP IS THE LANGUAGE, FOCUS, AND AMBIENT OF HEAVEN

The worship Father looks for goes far beyond our enthusiastic praise songs or our customary church practices. Though not bad in themselves, they may cloud our vision and expectations so that we stay comfortable with weaker expressions of Father's grand

"Abba" relationship with us. So by his Spirit, Father prepares us to practice on earth the very lifestyle that heaven enjoys.

Relationship once lost is now re-established. Worship once dead is now vibrant. Connecting relationship with worship, worship with relationship: to this end the Spirit of God ceaselessly, tirelessly reformats our mindset. In the awesome moment when we as children connect with our Father, at that moment all the covenantal promises, all El Shaddai's resources and all Father's pre-planned works penetrate from eternity and enter into time, from Father's heart to our hearts and we begin a process of change from one stage of glory to another. In relational worship Father's light shines out of darkness to give us the light of the knowledge of the glory of God—in the face of Christ (2 Corinthians 4:5).

> **God built into the flow of Scripture history a deliberate and measured rhythm for revealing who he is**

God built into the flow of Scripture history a deliberate and measured rhythm for revealing who he is. This progressive revelation, so different from the Western approach to history, is based on his own sovereignty and his purposes for humankind. God carefully selects the times, events and individuals to bear the burden of "revelation history" of his names that takes place in the context of human history. He intrudes into human history with his own agenda and for his own purposes.

His plan involves a fervent and ardent strategy for drawing men and women back into fellowship with himself. He moves through all human obstacles, physical and spiritual, as people permit him to touch their lives, in order to repair what has been damaged and broken. More than that, he takes the very brokenness that paralyzes his human creation, and enters into their brokenness to fashion the lifestyle that he originally intended with Adam and Eve in the garden.

Yet he does not simply restore what Adam and Eve lost in their Paradise. Rather, he builds a new and different way to relate to himself. Since his own nature resonates with the mended brokenness by Jesus' resurrection from the grave, Father now relates differently to people than he did to Adam. The brokenness of the filial bond that helped crush the life from Jesus on the cross (Psalm 22:1; Matthew 27:46; Mark 15:34) now stands healed and restored through the Spirit's life-giving work on Resurrection Sunday. With this purpose in mind, God has kept his own covenant and now provides the same life-giving Spirit to his offended wanderers. He now transforms the severed tie between himself and his estranged children into a vital, growing, and intimate relationship. All this "revelation history" started in the garden with the introduction of the dual relational name YHWH Elohim.

SELF-REVELATION AND SELF-AUTHENTICATION

God's self-revelation is a process by which he tells us who he is. He puts men and women into life situations and then he shows up. God has spoken "at many times and in various ways" (Hebrews 1:1) to a variety of biblical people: to leaders, patriarchs and prophets, and to others like Balaam. Into the flow of Scripture history, God chose to reveal himself methodically through his names to men: deliberately, carefully, through selected events or chosen people, with measured stages of information about himself, and for the purpose of restoring mankind to the place of interactive fellowship with himself. In the process of self-revelation, he has built in a delay factor for his

> **He transforms the severed tie into a vital, growing and intimate relationship**

own self-disclosure that is commonly referred to as "progressive revelation."

In the self-revelatory process, I want to suggest another phrase that complements self-revelation: self-authentication. I like it because it carries such a strong sense of God's authority and his purposes. The entire revelation of God from Genesis through Revelation is a strong process by which God is authenticating himself to the people, people groups and the nations they represent. Self-authentication is more than self-revelation; it has more to do with the deeds of God on earth. A primary example in the Old Testament is what God did to authenticate himself to Pharaoh, and the forces he brought to bear that stopped Pharaoh in his tracks. That's self-authentication. It fills out the term "self-revelation."

The primary act of self-authentication in the New Testament is the 3 ½ year stretch beginning with the time that Jesus came out of the wilderness and declared that the kingdom of God has come. He declared in essence, "It is here now in me." Then he went to Nazareth and made that great statement where he claimed Isaiah 61 for himself. He said, "The Spirit of the Lord is upon me because he has anointed me to preach good news to the poor," and so to carry on what Father gave him to do.

Self-authentication in the life of Jesus is found in the seven miracles in the book of John, starting in Cana where he turned water to wine and going on through to Resurrection Sunday. The self-authentication is seen on that Sunday morning when he got up. He shouldn't get up—he's dead! How can he get up, perfect and whole? That authenticates the name of YHWH Elohim El Shaddai, God Almighty, epitomized in the life of his own Son, Jesus of Nazareth, and continuing in the individual lives of the apostles as they took the gospel to the ends of the earth.

Introduction

God is saying, "This is who I Am," and he authenticates what he says by showing up on Earth through a display in power and authority that is reserved only for the living God. So our faith is based on two aspects of the revelatory process. The first aspect is that God speaks and reveals his heart to men and women through his names. The second aspect is that he steps into human history and authenticates his presence by adjusting the laws of physics here on earth to fit what he wants to do.

Father's Framework for Relational Worship

God's self-revelation through his names provides a framework for understanding his person and purposes on earth. This revelation comes in several ways. First, God reveals his names as recorded through oral literature. As Moses gave the creation account in Genesis 1-3, he used the name of God "Elohim" without any introduction, justification, or explanation. Moses just assumed that God self-exists, that all people know who he is, and that Elohim is his name.

A second way he reveals his name is to people directly: God tells them what his name is. For example, God names himself in Genesis 17:1 when the LORD appeared to Abram and told him that he is "El Shaddai, the Almighty." In Exodus 3:14, the LORD met Moses and told him that his name, forever, is "YHWH, the LORD."

God also reveals his names, especially in the Patriarchal Age, by the mouth of his servants. They used names not previously introduced in the Scriptures, but apparently known well enough that people recognized them as valid names for the One who is God. Melchizedek, in his encounter with Abram in Genesis 14, used God's name, "El Elyon, the Most High God." There is no previous use of this name in Scripture, but the author Moses recognized it and the authority it carried in the priest-king Melchizedek.

In addition, God reveals his names through experience, when people encounter him directly, both physically and emotionally. In effect, God leads people to know his name through the struggles they experience. Look at Jacob's wrestling with the Angel of the Lord in Genesis 32:22-32. After struggling all night with the Angel, Jacob recognized that God had revealed himself and he called the place Peniel, saying "It is because I saw God face to face."

Psalm 19 shows that God reveals his name as Creator through a multi-faceted creation, through the genetic code and innate atomic structure that declares unceasingly the glory of God; that is, his eternal power and divine nature. These invisible qualities call all people to account because they are "understood from what has been made" (Romans 1:20). In Acts 14:17, Paul states that "God has not left himself without testimony. He has shown kindness by giving you rain…he provides you with food…he fills your hearts with joy."

God reveals himself to every human on earth as Just and Judge through the "requirements of the law that are written on their hearts" People who do not have the Mosaic Law do by nature the things required by the Law, as described in Romans 2:14-15. Paul used this concept with the mainly Jewish congregation in Rome to establish his conviction that all humanity stands under judgment before God: They knew him as God but refused to acknowledge him and honor him as God.

Even with these avenues through which God has chosen to communicate his names, we still have only a partial view, at best an incomplete understanding of who he is. So God reserved the best for the last. He sent his only begotten, his one and only, the one who always lives "in the bosom of the Father" (John 1:18), to become a human being and communicate to us fully, completely, and finally just who God is. The name of God is seen in the face of Jesus Christ. Ponder with the disciple Philip his question and

INTRODUCTION

Jesus' response in John 14:9, "Don't you know me, Philip, even after I have been among you such a long time? Anyone who has seen me has seen the Father." The name of the unapproachable God is seen in the face of Jesus Christ. God displays the qualities of his own nature in the life, the work, the encounters, and sacrifice of Jesus of Nazareth, the Messiah-Servant.

FATHER'S INVITATION TO RELATIONAL WORSHIP

God chose these many diverse ways of progressive self-revelation as the vehicle for communicating his person, his nature, and above all, his compassionate purposes for humanity. Each name springs from a call to the filial relationship with Father-Son-Spirit. Let the encounter with each of his names meet you with an open heart to the person of God. Respond in awe that YHWH still comes in each of these ways today. He even incarnates himself in human flesh, yours and mine, in your culture and mine. He continues to come and reveal, to call and to claim. Consider how he has invited people into relationship and listen for the names he may yet speak to you.

> **Worship is not our initiative but rather our response to God's self-revealing presence and activity**

In the Scriptural revelation there are hundreds of names for God. This study will focus on a few primary names, the ones that God himself used to establish his person and purposes for all humanity. In Scripture, God initiates the worship process. He moves on us and awakens us in a surge, like a tsunami wave, to desire him, just as God did when he came daily and met with Adam and Eve in Eden. As participants in our egalitarian culture, with our self-actualizing mindset, we tend to assume that we can worship God on our own initiative whenever we wish. However, the reality is that worship is only possible through God's initiative: the Spirit's wooing work by means of the blood sacrifice of Jesus at Calvary.

The longer we travel on our faith-journey by the Spirit, the more we become aware that God permeates our daily existence. God is no respecter of location, home, business, or church. He touches our lives with invitations to recognize and know him as a father knows his own child. The names of God serve to prepare us as Father's children to respond to Father's initiative. If we, as believing worshipers, can bring the names of God into our immediate and daily experiences—home, business, church—then we bring Father's rulership to earth. The meaning, authority, and power of his names transform mere natural existence into an opportunity to bring Father's compassionate reign into our lives and the lives of those around us.

OUR WORSHIP RESPONSE

Worship is not our initiative but rather our response to God's self-revealing presence and activity. Our goal is that God might infuse our human spirit with the Spirit of God, to allow us to worship and fellowship with him interactively, to experience together the manifest presence of God. Worship means to enter the pathway prepared by the Spirit who leads us to Jesus. Then Jesus takes us by our hand and together we walk into Father's presence. Worship is a progressive drawing into the heart of God. Ask him to awaken all that is within you to respond to him. As you prepare your heart to worship him, the following heart attitudes can help you enter into fellowship and worship of the Living God as our reasonable response to his Spirit's initiative.

> **Worship is in fact our entire day's work**

INTRODUCTION

Worship is in fact our entire day's work. From the moment we awake and arise and begin to engage the duties of the day, at that point we can step into worship in the Hebrew sense of the word worship. In English it is translated praise and adoration. But more than that, in Hebrew, worship has to do with the work you are doing, the work of your hands, the work of your mind. It is worship to the Living God. We worship with our words and our voice, yes. And we go to work, and there we worship him there in that sense of worship.

Each of the following heart attitudes is a starting point in developing a normal approach to God in worship as you learn his self-revealed names. Each believer will come to appreciate God from his and her own perspective, genetic structure, life's experiences, and work, as well as the Spirit's gifting, for God expects and encourages a unique approach in worship from each one of his unique believers.

I OPEN to receive his presence and word. My heart, soul, mind, and strength are alert to respond to his presence.

I BOW AND YIELD my heart/soul/mind/strength to him. Jesus reiterates the great command from the Lord, through Moses, to "love YHWH your Elohim with all your heart, with all your soul, with all your strength, and with all your mind" (Luke 10:27 quoting from Deuteronomy 6:5). This means to yield my entire self to him and open my entire self for hearing and following his words.

I MEDITATE on the name in focus, who he is. I take this name and declare my worship of him who reveals himself by this name. I meditate on the meaning of the name and its placement in God's unfolding self-revelation.

I REFLECT on the actions or events associated with this name. I review the various people, events, and teachings associated with this name, noting how he responds to my worship. The name in its context helps define the full meaning of the name. I learn to be sensitive to the information that surrounds the appearance of his various names in Scripture. God introduces his name in the setting of people, events, and teachings, giving us the privilege of following him in his self-unfolding to humanity.

I APPLY the significance of his name to my life. This name tells me who he is and what he wants me to do today. In the light of this name, I ask him how he is going to change me so that the significance of his name becomes part of my mindset and lifestyle. What does he want me to do today that will reflect the content of this name?

I REMEMBER my neighbor. To love the Lord my God means to love the people around me as myself. Complete the injunction of Luke 10:27 from Deuteronomy 6:5 and Leviticus 19:18 by applying the healing expectations of his name and his activities to the people around me, to those I love so deeply.

I FOCUS ON JESUS, THE LIVING WORD. YHWH Jesus is now your wisdom, your righteousness, your holiness, and your redemption (I Corinthians 1:30). Let his Word fill your being, a Word that vivifies you, a Word that strengthens you, a Word that clarifies your understanding, a Word that emphasizes a previous exhortation to you, a Word that directs you into new meditation or activity. Perhaps a Word will come up into your heart just now or perhaps you will detect just his presence. But his promise states that no eye has seen, no ear has heard, no mind has conceived (that is, it has not come up into, it has not occurred to the heart of man) what God has prepared for those who love him. (I Corinthians 2:9). It is in this posture of worship-adoration that the Word of God comes up into our hearts. We see, understand, and comprehend his feelings and purposes for us in the overflow of his Spirit and presence.

Introduction

I ENTER into God's Presence, into the worship of YHWH Elohim with thanksgiving, praise, and adoration. Sometimes Father's presence comes in a hush. Then we wait for more of him. Sometimes Father's presence comes in a moment of rush. Then he is saying, "Now get on this. I've talked to you about this many times and I want you to do it." And between these two extremes is the whole gamut of waiting on the Lord. We wait on the Presence as we flow through all of these areas of worshiping YHWH. It's an endless process that Father delights to teach us, tutor us, nurture us in the practice of worship. I acknowledge his worthiness, holiness, goodness, and faithfulness: my Lord and my God!

I REST IN HIS PRESENCE, IN HIM COMPLETE. This is totally contrary to the rationalism in the western world of the last eight centuries and totally contrary to the modern lifestyle that attempts to spread itself all over the world. Nobody is resting. Everybody is striving to make his own place. Rest flows out of the Father through Jesus Christ in the Holy Spirit. They are all expert at resting. Learn from them how to worship. Then rest in your worship. YHWH's Presence means rest.

As you prepare your heart to worship him, may these heart attitudes help you enter into fellowship and worship of the Living God as our reasonable response to his Spirit's initiative. He is holy and he is worthy!

Section One

Worshiping YHWH in the Adamic Era

We can only imagine how often and for what space of time Adam and Eve came together in the garden to share life through the ongoing, stunning discoveries of all that God had built into the Garden of Eden, the unresolved issues before them in naming animals and cultivating the Garden, as well as God's own thoughts and as yet unrealized heartfelt purposes. Elohim's presence abided over and permeated the Garden in its entirety. This is the norm: God living among his people.

We will not find in Scripture a detailed listing of the worship practices that YHWH gave directly to the first couple and family. But YHWH found worshipers, and these worship practices can be inferred by watching them as they related to God directly.

The first example of worship is in the grain and animal sacrifices that Abel and Cain brought to YHWH. Apparently, they realized that sacrifices would please YHWH Elohim. However, the remainder of Scripture interprets for us the issue before YHWH: he loved Abel and his sacrifice and hated Cain and his sacrifice (Genesis 4:4,5). Hebrews 11:4 tells us that Abel offered God a better sacrifice because he approached by faith.

Hebrews 11:6 clarifies that "without faith it is impossible to please God." This faith principle operates in all situations with all peoples, irrespective of when they lived on earth, starting in the Garden of Eden. To walk with God as a child with one's father is what gives the content of faith and defines the word "worship."

A second example of worship and faith during this era surrounds the little that is known about Enoch of the lineage from Adam to Seth. The text leaves us to infer that YHWH Elohim deeply appreciated the way that Enoch approached and related to him in faith—so much so that YHWH simply took Enoch home to be with him, without passing through the human experience of death.

In Genesis 6:3, God said, "My Spirit will not contend with man forever." He saw that every inclination of the thoughts of their hearts was only evil all the time. And the LORD was grieved and his heart was filled with pain: pain on losing the filial relationship, the regular fellowship with those made in his own image, pain at seeing their ruined souls increasingly polluted and yet perversely insistent on spreading their own poison to as many as possible. The loss became so great to YHWH that he determined to wipe out the entire race, the most beloved part of creation: those created for worship were now bent on dishonoring God in every way they could.

So now, think about how Noah found favor in the eyes of the Lord. Under the generational mantle of faith-worship, Noah stood out among all peoples on earth as pleasing to the Lord. The writer of Hebrews says that he built the ark in "holy fear." This is a life-giving awe that stems from appreciating the holiness of God. The practice of bowing to God, honoring and thanking him, releases to us this appreciation. As we live in this worshiping filial bond of relationship, we realize more and more the purity and excellence of God. So by faith Noah's life condemned the unbelieving world and he became heir of the righteousness that comes by faith.

Throughout the Adamic Era, it is clear that God built into all created humans a faith-response that he expects them to exercise toward himself. That faith-response towards God results in worship, a normal and continual expression of thankfulness towards God, based on an awareness of God's constant provision and one's dependency on him. The deeper our consciousness of God's faithful care, the deeper we worship. Equally, the deeper our awareness of reliance on him, the deeper we worship.

As we read Genesis 1-11, we encounter these three names: (1) Elohim, (2) YHWH-Elohim, and (3) YHWH. The most accurate and productive method for studying God's names is to look at the Hebrew approach of experiencing life when and where the names of God are revealed. We want to know the real contexts in which his name is used and the encounters in which God tells human beings what his name is. Our foundation for understanding his names lies in the Biblical text and the human history that surrounds these revelational events and encounters. So we will look at the biblical text, as well as the meaning indicated in the original Hebrew.

Chapter One

ELOHIM, THE ONE WHO BEGINS EVERYTHING

Come, meet, and focus on the one who is the source and object of biblical worship in the Adamic era by looking at the name Elohim. As followers of Jesus, our goal is to know God, who he is, his nature, his purposes, and above all, how to worship him so that we can bring him joy and fulfill his purposes on earth.

> **Imagine yourself back at the incredible awe-inspiring moment when God simply spoke and our vast universe came into being**

To understand the context for how Moses used the name Elohim as God's basic name in Genesis 1, you must know the time and context when YHWH Elohim shared this name with him. Evangelical scholars consider Moses' 40 days on Mt. Sinai as the time and context when YHWH shared with him both the creation background of Adam through Abraham, as well as the Covenant Law for Israel, including the Ten Commandments. Moses heard directly from YHWH all the details of life on earth up to Moses' time.

ENCOUNTERING ELOHIM

Imagine yourself back at the incredible awe-inspiring moment when God simply spoke and our vast universe came into being. Moses introduces the narrative with these words: "In the beginning God (Elohim) created the heavens and the earth" (Genesis 1:1). Moses made no definition of who God is, no statement of his person, authority, or power. He just assumed that God "is" and that God is the one responsible for the existence of this entire universe. Then Moses began the detailed account of just how God went about creating the various stages of planetary, plant, animal, and human creation.

Throughout the creation account are embedded the worship attitudes and practices that permeate the living context of the initial families in the Adamic Era. There are no detailed instructions from God on how to worship him. Rather, there are on-going stories of what people did as they approached and related to God in filial relationship, either to worship him or ignore him.

Encountering and Worshiping Elohim through the Creation Mandate

In the Genesis account of creation, God instructed Adam on ways to relate to him and worship him with a deep filial bond. Evangelical commentators refer to this set of instructions as the "Creation Mandate." First, Elohim created the human as male and female. Then he blessed them and said to them in Genesis 1:28:

- Be fruitful and increase in number [multiply by families];
- Fill the earth [spread out to cover the entire earth by families];
- Subdue it [learn to comprehend the structure, function and purpose for each creature, not subjugate or destroy];
- Rule over all the creatures of the air, water, and ground [control growth for productivity, not exploitation].

"Worship" in a broad sense is to carry out the instructions and ways of God. The first relational worship experiences included the following areas that comprise worship inherent in the creation mandate.

WORK. God, in Hebrew "Elohim," created the Garden of Eden and put Adam to work it and take care of it (Genesis 2:8). Elohim gave instructions to farm the Garden of Eden, to till the soil, care for the trees and shrubs, and to understand and name the animal life. At this point Elohim created Eve out of Adam's side to be a "suitable helper" to help him on their journey through life.

Any person who lacks Elohim's perspective on work may view work as a domineering tyrant, a cultural artifact or a way to exalt the worker. The various pharaohs owned and expended their workers; communism affects to exalt workers in order to take control of their own countries; socialism takes most of the workers' wages in return for paying their womb-to-tomb expenses; capitalism cultivates extraordinary salaries for some workers, while squeezing the efforts of others. But from the beginning of human activity, Elohim gave his worker increasing responsibility and abundant resources, balanced by effective accountability.

REST DAY. From the first creation account (Genesis 2:2-3) Elohim instructed Adam to rest one day in seven, to refrain from all normal work, even as Elohim himself "rested from all the work of creating" on the seventh day. One who works a seven-day week and ignores the biblical rest-day builds intolerable stress levels while eventually being crippled with physical ailments and premature death.

MARRIAGE. Elohim sketched a shadow-type of his own complex identity by instructing Adam and Eve on how to handle the marriage situation. A man leaves his own father and mother and joins himself with his wife so that they become one person, one flesh before Elohim. But the oneness is far more than physical; the physical melds into a joining of spirits, those of the husband, wife, and himself, indeed a shadow type for God's complex and triune self.

Ephesians 5:22-32 outlines the purpose and format for marriage: husbands are to love their wives as Christ loves the church and wives are to yield to their husbands, as the church yields to Christ. To view marriage only as a "social contract" for the benefit of society effectively removes from the couple their God-given and heaven-designed gift of human oneness and thus keeps them from seeing the underlying reality of the Triune God in all the complexity of Father-Son-Spirit.

OFFERINGS. Somewhere in the flow of creation instructions, Elohim created in the human the awareness that one can also worship God through offerings. Though not recorded as direct instructions from Elohim, Genesis 4:2-5 tells us that Adam's children approached God by means of offerings: Abel with animals from his flocks and Cain with grains from his cultivated fields.

Elohim rejected Cain's offerings and received Abel's offerings. The reason lies not in the materials offered in sacrifice, animals versus grains, but in the attitude with which both men approached God with their offerings. Cain's angry reaction to Elohim elicited this penetrating response: "If you do what is right, will you not be accepted? But if you do not do what is right, sin is crouching at your door. It desires to have you, but you must master it" (Genesis 4:6-7). Cain already knew right from wrong and nevertheless approached Elohim with self-centered attitudes and motives, whereas Abel came to God in yielded faith and trust. Cain believed he had the right to offer God what pleased Cain. Devoid of thanksgiving, he yielded to the spirit of sin instead of mastering it. "And on Cain and his offering God did not look with favor" (Genesis 4:5). In contrast, Abel approached Elohim with offerings and an attitude of worship that he knew was pleasing to God.

The natural human approach says "I will take to Elohim what I want." As then, so also now: those who retain the right to treat God as they wish soon develop a powerful motive to justify their own actions and destroy those who differ. This is the spirit of independence and self-fulfillment and god-playing that permeates humanism in today's world, and puts today's believer at the same risk as Cain's.

THANKSGIVING. One who abandons offerings to God, of whatever sort, as a lifetime practice is placed in the same position as the one who never gives thanks to God. That person comes to think of him or herself as the center of the universe, without accountability to the living God. As lack of thanksgiving leads to idolatry of other things, so also lack of offerings lead to idolatry of self.

Many centuries later Paul the Apostle brought clarity to the importance of thanksgiving. Romans 1:21-25 explains how people who know God and decide not to honor him nor thank him have their minds touched by Elohim so that their thinking becomes futile (useless) and their minds dark (unable to know God). They exchange the glory of God for images that look like men or animals, thereby exchanging the truth about God for a lie. To refrain from giving thanks leads to idolatry that in turn leads to unrestrained immorality.

In these issues of work, rest, marriage, offerings, and thanksgiving, one can see that worship issues from people who willingly honor and please their Creator. To obey him is to please him and to please him is to worship him. In other words, obedience is inherent in worship and worship is inherent in obedience. This theme permeates life on earth; it is Elohim's perspective for enjoying life on earth with his people: obedience is worship and worship is obedience. A.W. Tozer says it so eloquently in *The Pursuit of God*, "The worshiping heart does not create its Object. It finds him here when it awakes from its moral slumber in the morning of its regeneration."

The Name Elohim

The word-root in Hebrew for Elohim is El and signifies "power." The predominant use of the term Elohim means "the God of power," as we see in Genesis 1:1. This is the name for God first found in Genesis. Hundreds of verses in the Old Testament use this name, with almost a bewildering array of contexts and inferences. Here are a few of the contextual meanings for Elohim that you can use for on-going worship. Your sensitivity to other uses of this name will build into your spirit a far deeper appreciation for who he is as Elohim.

ELOHIM—GOD WHO HAS TOTAL POWER AND IS ALWAYS THERE. Our English translation is typically "God." When we use the term "God," in English, we have a vague awareness of "the-God-who-is-there," much like the New Testament term "theos" in Greek. In contrast, the name "God" in vernacular English often means whatever the speaker wishes it to mean. Notice that in Genesis 1, there is no explanation for where he comes from, no philosophical justification for why he should or shouldn't exist. He is just there! **This is the one who will always be there for you. Let this one who is inexplicably and inextricably there become the object of your worship.**

ELOHIM—GOD WHO EXISTS BEFORE AND APART FROM OUR UNIVERSE. This self-existing God is the ground of all existence. He has been recognized and named among countless tribal and aboriginal groups across the face of earth. In folklore accounts, they have applied numerous names to him but have never known or personally come to relate with him. They know him through creation; they know his presence in the silent forest, the roaring waves and the majestic mountains. But they feel he does not talk to them in a self-revelatory manner. They are left to project by inference and analogy, trance and dance, just who he is. In Native American traditions, they call him the "Great Spirit." One particular group in the northwest U.S. named him the "Thundering Silence," for they perceived his presence in the oceans and forests. But he never came to them and introduced himself in a series of names or expressed what he wanted for them. Look at the folklore from many aboriginal groups on earth, and you will find the One-Who-Self-Exists. He has no beginning and, apparently, he has no end. No one created him, nor did he develop himself into being God. He exists, based on his own resources, means, and purposes.

> **The self-existing God has no beginning and no end**

He was alive before all things existed. There never was a time when he did not exist. There never will be a time when he does not exist. He created our space-time continuum and lives outside it, not dependent on it. He intrudes upon our earthly life according to his mission and goals. **This is the one who knows you and is the source of your existence.**

ELOHIM—GOD WHO IS SPIRIT. Later on in Exodus 33:20, Moses explains to readers that God has no physical body; he is spirit. Moses quotes God as saying, "you cannot see my face, for no one may see me and live." John 1:12 says, "No one has ever seen God, but God the Only Begotten, who is at Father's side, he has made him known." Jesus also says in John 4:24 that "God is spirit and his worshipers must worship him in spirit and in truth," and in John 6:46, Jesus says, "No one has seen the Father except the one who is from God; only he has seen the Father." Paul says in 1 Timothy 1:17 that the "king is eternal, immortal, *invisible.*" In 1 Timothy 6:15 he proclaims that "...God, the blessed and only Ruler, the King of kings and Lord of lords, who alone is immortal and who lives in unapproachable light, whom no one has seen or can see." **This is the one who loves your worship.**

ELOHIM—GOD WHO CREATES. He makes all things out of nothing. He orders and arranges all things he creates. He created our space-time continuum, but lives outside of its confines. This universe he created depends entirely on him for existence; in no way does he depend on the universe for his own existence. He regularly intrudes to accomplish his purposes.

The writer to the Hebrews states in 11:3, "By faith we understand that the universe was formed at God's command, so that what is seen was not made out of what was visible." In Hebrew the word *barah*, as seen in Genesis 1:1, means "to create." The word *barah* in its several contexts, makes no mention of God using a previous creation or resources to make this one in which we live. Therefore commentators usually translate the word as "create, to make out of nothing."

Now there are other words in Hebrew for make, such as "fashion" or "form" that suggest the use of materials previously existing, but that is not the case in Genesis where God created abundantly and then in 1:27 it tells us, "So God created man in his own image, in the image of God he created him; male and female he created them." In Genesis 5:1-2 we are told "When God created man, he made him in the likeness of God. He created them male and female and blessed them. And when they were created, he called them 'man'" (often referred to as mankind). **This is the one who knows your every cell and thought because he created you** (Psalm 139).

ELOHIM—GOD WHO HAS UNLIMITED RESOURCES. Elohim-Who-Is-Limitless creates out of his own resources, which are unlimited. His power is behind our ever-expanding universe. He calls on no one to help him exist or create. He makes no use of materials other than what is within himself. There is no limit on his presence, that is, his omnipresence. There is no limit on his power, for he is omnipotent and his knowledge is omniscient. Psalm 147 declares, "Great is the Lord and mighty in power; his understanding has no limit." **This is the one who fathers you and provides for you.**

ELOHIM—GOD WHO HAS LIFE IN HIMSELF. Elohim is the one who is alive out of his own resources. He depends on no one else for life—his or anyone else's. Jesus speaks of him as the "Father who raises the dead and gives them life" (John 5:21). Jesus calls him "the One who has life in himself" (John 5:26). Paul speaks of him in reference to Abraham's commitment to him as "the God who gives life to the dead and calls things that are not, as though they exist" (Romans 4:17). **This is the one who pours his own life into you.**

> **Our yieldedness opens the door to the Presence of God**

ELOHIM—GOD WHO MAKES COVENANTS. In Hebrew, the term covenant, or *berith*, is a God-initiated arrangement that binds the receiver to himself and provides life, resources, and purpose for life on earth to all who receive him. In Genesis 1 through 3 we find the rudiments of a covenant. God makes a specific arrangement with Adam and Eve on how to live in the garden, then later on how to live under the curse for disobedience. God always arranges covenants when he deals with mankind. God laid out his purposes and asked the man and woman to cooperate with him in the working out of those purposes. The further we go in revelational history, the more complex and redemptive are the covenants he makes with Noah, Abraham, Moses, David, and the prophets. In Jesus of Nazareth, Father's quintessential covenant person is revealed. His redemptive work and resources cover all mankind – all who come to him by faith. **This is the one who guarantees your place in his family.**

Worshiping YHWH as Elohim

YIELD. Bow your heart/soul/mind/strength to Elohim; that is, yield your entire self to him. Open yourself to receive his presence and his word. Meditate on his name: Elohim. To yield means that the penitent man or woman bows before his Lord in his heart all day and night and in his physical form when it is appropriate. Our yieldedness opens the door to the Presence of God.

We notice God's Presence and then we yield to him and open our hearts. That's usually how it works. But yieldedness is the key note of the penitent brother or sister in Christ. Penitent simply means repentance. Repent means turn around and go the other way. And the yieldedness that is needed for that is indeed a distinct gift of God.

GIVE THANKS. Thank Elohim for all he has done in your life. Review all his powerful and wondrous acts or deeds that come to mind, those that have touched your life and those that have touched others. Recall each day's accomplishment in gratitude. Use appropriate Psalms to aid you in recognizing his deeds. For instance, take Psalm 103:1-5 as a model for remembering specifically and in detail God's goodness to you.

PRAISE. Enumerate before him, Elohim, all his characteristics, his qualities as a person, such as his limitless power, his faithfulness, any of his characteristics you have discovered in reading this chapter and in Scripture. Use Scripture such as Psalm 19 and 103 to declare and praise Elohim's goodness.

ADORE. Continue in thanksgiving and praise until you sense the first stirrings of his presence, the presence of Elohim. This is not soulish, self-centered or abstract worship. Declare your relational love and adoration of Elohim who loves you beyond measure. Gradually move into silence as you sense Elohim's presence come alongside yours. Wait in silence by quieting your mind and the strident demands of your soul. This discipline will become a habit that becomes easier with repeated practice.

Worship and Become Aware of His Presence. The Psalmist says, "Be still and know that I am God." Be quiet and wait until you come to realize or comprehend that he is Elohim. Gradually Elohim's presence begins to permeate your mind, soul, and spirit. You know that he is God! The closer his presence comes, the more we grow silent. His presence stills our voice as we sense the awe of his presence.

Wait for Him to Share His Heart. Since Scripture tells us of how God has pursued us for years, desiring that we fellowship with him, we expect him to begin to share his heart with us, to unfold to us his purposes, his works, his opinions on our situations, and especially his loving care over us. Let the Spirit bring to mind and heart the appropriate Scripture that pertains to you, your work for him, or words that interpret life for you, the unresolved situation, the point of suffering, the unknown step that lies ahead, so that Elohim might share with you his perspective and solution. Just wait in his presence for his touch on you.

Chapter Two

YHWH Elohim, the Powerful and Relational One Who Self-Exists

In the second creation account, in Genesis 2:4 through 3:24, the narrative introduces his dual name, YHWH Elohim. It comes with no explanation for the name change from Elohim in Genesis 1. YHWH Elohim reveals God as one who relates with people, the humans whom he made in his own image. As Elohim, the Powerful One who self-exists, he amply demonstrated his inimitable, infinite power and wisdom in creating our space-time universe. But in the second creation account as YHWH Elohim, he enters into an interactive relationship with his created humans, first with Adam, and then with Eve.

The Purposes of YHWH Elohim in the Creation of Man

We see God's purposes in the Scriptural declaration that YHWH Elohim made the heavens and the earth, and there was no man to work the land. God purposed to create the heavens and the earth as a place where Adam could work the ground (Genesis 2:4-5). After YHWH Elohim created Adam, he placed him in a garden he had planted specifically for Adam to cultivate. After creation, there were surprisingly no cultivated grains or "shrubs of the field," as no rain had yet watered the earth and no man had worked the land.

Then God made all kinds of trees to grow in this garden. Here he took Adam, his created masterpiece, and placed him in the garden to work it and make it produce by caring for it. He also made two outstanding and exceptional trees. One he named the "tree of life" (literally, the tree that gives life), and the other he named "the tree of the knowledge of good and evil" (literally, the tree that gives the knowledge of good and evil).

Scripture does not detail for us what this special tree had in its fruit that would give one the knowledge and capacity for determining good and evil. Apparently, Adam was to depend upon YHWH Elohim for his evaluations and conclusions about moral or ethical issues, thereby learning God's own perspective and mindset about morality. YHWH Elohim then began to practice his relationship with Adam by sharing two things with him: responsibility and accountability, even as he does with us today.

He did not give to Adam the capacity to create new species or new worlds, but he did give the commission to care for what he had made (Genesis 2:15). Adam's work was to take responsibility to cultivate the garden on behalf of YHWH Elohim. And God surrounded the man with well-defined parameters of accountability. Adam was never to eat from the tree of the knowledge of good and evil because, if he did so, he would surely and permanently die. But the life-tree in the midst of the garden had no such restrictions. Adam could eat anything in the garden except the fruit of the knowledge-tree.

> **YHWH Elohim built his creation for his own purpose of relating with it as the high point of his created universe**

Adam's delegated responsibility also included naming all the birds and animals that YHWH Elohim brought to him (Genesis 2:19).

YHWH Elohim, the Powerful and Relational One Who Self-Exists

Whatever name Adam discerned as the essence or purpose for that animal, "that was its name." God accepted Adam's choices as the names for birds and animals he would use for them.

But for both Adam and the Creator, the work was still incomplete for Adam had no one with whom to share life on a human level, to share his own vulnerability and limitations. YHWH Elohim made a moral choice and declared this to be "not good" and set about to produce the woman, the one who was suitable or appropriate for Adam. At the point of Adam's vulnerability, a rib that protects the heart, he fashioned the woman and called her Eve or "living," for she would become the mother of all those who lived after her.

These actions display the characteristics of the name YHWH Elohim and show how YHWH Elohim built his creation for his own purpose of relating with it as the high point of his created universe. Through his relationship with Adam and Eve, YHWH Elohim displayed his great plan of the ages for all creation.

Encountering YHWH Elohim

Genesis 3 records that the man and his wife heard the sound of YHWH Elohim as he was walking in the garden in the cool of the day. The LORD God loved the practice of sharing life together in this setting. For this very reason YHWH Elohim had called the universe into existence—our space-time continuum—for the purpose of living with men and women and enjoying life together in the great garden he provided for them.

In Genesis 3, in the account of Eve and the serpent it is interesting to note that the serpent used the name Elohim but not YHWH Elohim, avoiding the focus of the God who calls us to relationship. He questions the woman with "Has God indeed said...." And Eve agrees that God/Elohim gave that command. Then they "heard the sound of the LORD God/ YHWH Elohim walking in the garden, and Adam and his wife hid themselves from the presence of the LORD God." They knew they had disobeyed and lost a precious part of the chosen relationship YHWH Elohim had desired and they hid from the relational God who makes covenant.

> **His cry, "Where are you?" is a realization of the awful consequences of the couple's choice to manage life on their own terms**

Now imagine the scenario. Both Adam and Eve had come to recognize the "sound" flowing from the presence of YHWH Elohim. But on this day, that sound brought dread to their hearts and they hid because they had opted to choose life on their own terms instead of listening to YHWH Elohim's life-giving counsel. Although as omniscient God he knew this tragedy would unfold, as Father he cried out!

His cry, "Where are you?" is hardly a request for information as to their location. Rather, God realized the awful consequences already set in motion by the couple's choice to manage life on their own terms. As Father, he cried out because his child was missing, gone, like a child willfully entering an animal's den and facing mauling and death. YHWH Elohim's heart-cry came from the broken promise and commitment given to him by Adam and Eve and from the disastrous results soon to be visited on the couple. Most of all, he cried out because he had lost the very relationship for which he had designed the entire creation—with humans as the apex of all life in the universe.

Ever since that day in the Garden, YHWH Elohim has continued, with all his resources, to pursue his wounded friends who have little or no awareness of the relationship lost. From that day in the Garden, YHWH Elohim carried a wounded heart, a sad-

YHWH Elohim, the Powerful and Relational One Who Self-Exists

dened spirit because he had lost what was most valuable to him. He yearned over his broken and devastated humanity. The greatness of his own loss is only matched by the greatness of the solution he provided in his own son, his one and only. His only begotten son entered the human arena to experience for himself a broken and lost relationship with YHWH Elohim, his own Father, and paid the awesome cost of the broken relationship the first couple perpetrated. The crushing experience of the cross fit the anguish and assuaged it, the anguish that YHWH Elohim carried over the broken bond with those he created and loved.

He redeems, provides the means, and pays the costs for renovating what has been ruined. He restores all things he makes. Because of this loss and the cost willingly paid by Jesus, God's unspeakable joy at the resurrection of his son can only be imagined, especially at the ascension, the return of his lost son and the mending of the lost relationship with humankind. Now and for all time and eternity, Father stands reconciled. He has restored friendship and filial relationship again with all humanity. We are his family and sons and daughters! Any and all may embrace this restored relationship with Father. All this came as a result of Jesus' willingness to pay the cost.

The Name YHWH Elohim

The word YHWH in Hebrew comes from a most common verb, the verb "to be." At the point of God's self-revelation in Genesis, he tells us nothing about the source for his name or how to use it. God preserved the self-revelation process by not explaining the name YHWH until the Mosaic description of YHWH's name in Exodus 3:14. Moses used the YHWH name for the earlier parts of Scripture because he had come to comprehend its significance in the Mt. Sinai experience. Therefore, in Genesis 2 and 3 we find the name used, but without explanation. In Exodus 3:15 we find out that God preferred the use of his name YHWH, when he declared, "This is my name forever, the name by which I am to be remembered from generation to generation."

The differentiation between the names Elohim and YHWH is drawn from the contextual use of these names, not from the meaning of the Hebrew words themselves, where Elohim means God and YHWH means Lord. Chapter 1 focuses on Elohim while chapters 2-11 focus on the occurrences of his double name YHWH Elohim, not the individual name of Elohim.

Now let's reflect on who YHWH is, the God whose gracious heart purposes to fellowship with humans.

YHWH ELOHIM – GOD WHO WANTS TO REPRESENT HIMSELF ON EARTH THROUGH HUMANS. This is the God who created you and wants to represents himself through you.

YHWH ELOHIM – GOD WHO CREATES EARTH AND PEOPLE FOR SPECIFIC PURPOSES. This is the God who created you in the womb (Psalm 139), gave you your specific DNA, that you might fulfill his specific purposes just for you.

YHWH ELOHIM – GOD WHO PROVIDES FOR HUMAN NEEDS. This is the God who will provide all your needs. This is the God who taught us to pray, "Give us today our daily bread." He is the one who will bring to you all you need for this day.

YHWH ELOHIM – GOD WHO PROVIDES FOR UNLIMITED LIFE IN THE MIDST OF PRODUCTIVE WORK. Just like Jesus received unlimited life in the midst of the work Father gave him to do, so he has life and productive work for you. This is the God who preplanned for you to be holy and blameless in his sight and to be conformed to the Image of his son Jesus (Ephesians 1:4-10).

YHWH ELOHIM – GOD WHO DEFINES PARAMETERS FOR LIFE AND WORK. Adam and Eve were both given specific things to do, with limitations that would draw their hearts to YHWH Elohim. This is the God who recognizes your every limitation, defines your parameters, and walks with you in your life and work until the day He brings you home.

> **God determines the times set for us and the exact places where we should live**

YHWH ELOHIM – GOD WHO GIVES HUSBANDS AND WIVES AS MUTUAL HELPERS. This is the God who knew who your family would be, whether it would include a husband or wife, or a spiritual family. He knows you need a helper and that's why he sent his Holy Spirit to walk with us each day.

YHWH ELOHIM – GOD WHO GIVES CHILDREN AND GRANDCHILDREN. This is the God who has the generational plan for the ages designed for you. He populates his earth with his goodness. Children and grandchildren are his gift as are each and every one of your spiritual family.

YHWH ELOHIM – GOD WHO GIVES PLACEMENT, FOOD, AND CLOTHES. This is the God who knows where you are and what you need and has promised to provide all the specifics of life. Acts 17:26-27 says: "From one man he made every nation of men, that they should inhabit the whole earth, and he determined the times set for them and the exact places where they should live. God did this so that men would seek him and perhaps reach out for him and find him, though he is not far from each one of us." God placed you where you are so that you too would seek him and find him.

YHWH ELOHIM – GOD WHO PERMITS SATAN TO TEST COMMITMENT AND RELATIONSHIP. This is the God who permitted Satan to test Adam and Eve and who also allows you to be tested.

It is why Jesus taught us to pray, "Lead us not into temptation, but deliver us from the evil one."

Worshiping YHWH as YHWH Elohim

Worshiping God as YHWH Elohim is the outflow of relationship with the God of the universe, both powerful and relational. In worshiping God as YHWH Elohim, let thanksgiving, praise, adoration, and worship around his name arise from within you.

Thank YHWH Elohim for all he has done. Begin with offering thanks for YHWH-Elohim's creation: (1) the uniqueness of humans created in his image, (2) the entire spectrum of creation with animals and fish, trees and bushes, stars and galaxies, and the original eco-system from his hand, (3) the Tree of Life in the middle of the garden, (4) the relationship he established between man, woman, and himself, (5) the work that he gave to Adam, (6) the creation of woman as a helper suitable for Adam with the gift of children, and (7) permitting Satan access to the garden and the Tree of Knowledge to test the commitment of those he made in his own image. Continue with your own items of thanksgiving to add to these.

Praise and Adore YHWH Elohim for his profound beauty and virtue. Ask the Spirit to share with you the characteristics of his beauty and virtue (Psalm 27:4). His entire creation projects the Creator's nature in exquisite detail and overwhelming grandeur. Share these with YHWH Elohim directly. Begin to wait in increasing silence for his presence.

Worship YHWH Elohim. Let your adoration of YHWH Elohim blend into your heartfelt worship of him. Pour the love of your heart, soul, mind, and strength into his presence being with Him. Let it be like a poured out sacrifice of the best you are and have, permanently released to him. He takes that sacrifice and transmutes it into a word for you, a sharing of himself in appreciation for your love for him.

YHWH Elohim, the Powerful and Relational One Who Self-Exists

Wait for YHWH Elohim. He deeply desires to share himself with you. Become like an expectant child waiting for his father's word, for his sharing. 2 Peter 1:4 clarifies that through his great and precious promises we come to "participate in the divine nature and escape the corruption and decay in the world caused by evil desires." Remember he has assured you that through his word you will imbibe, absorb, and assimilate the person and nature of YHWH Elohim.

SECTION TWO

WORSHIPING YHWH IN THE ABRAHAMIC ERA

Note: In Genesis we learn that Abram's name was changed to Abraham and similarly Sarai became Sarah. Since they are known as Abraham and Sarah in most of the rest of Scripture, we will also call them by those names here.

Abraham's spiritual life is an outflow of his filial relationship with YHWH, expressed in the names that God revealed to him. His natural life by contrast is set in the context of the Mid-Eastern cultures in the second millennium B.C. From the Scriptures we watch the melding of two great rivers of history: human history and salvation history. God intrudes into Mid-Eastern history to initiate his own plans for drawing to himself his selfishly-oriented and wandering people. He breaks in to speak with them by using his names, with covenants modeled on the ancient Hittite culture.

Abraham was a wandering Hittite, native of Babylonia, a wealthy businessman. Over many years he traveled the trade routes of the Fertile Crescent with his family and his flock, finally arriving at the very mountain where one day the Son of God would pour out his life for our sin. Abraham received covenant words directly from YHWH and built many altars to demonstrate to everyone that he was a worshiper of YHWH. Though Scripture clearly shows Abraham's penchant for shading the truth, YHWH protected him and multiplied his assets.

YHWH first spoke to Abraham in vision form while he was still in Mesopotamia, Ur of the Chaldees, before he arrived in Haran (Genesis 15:7 and Acts 7:2). YHWH told Abraham to leave his country and people and go to the land that he would show him. God had several societies where he could have intruded to make known and initiate his salvation plans. Perhaps he chose Abraham in Ur of the Chaldees, a city in Babylonia, to bring redemption out of the ashes of Babel -- the attempt that failed to build a tower-structure that would reach to and control heaven itself. Basically, God wanted to build his own city, establish his own sovereign rule, and people it with those who loved and trusted him. So quite definitely, he ordered Abraham, whom he trusted, to leave Babylonia with his family and resources.

> **God has set the stage socially, politically and culturally for the next phase of his salvation history**

Abraham, undaunted by a lack of specific destination, left Ur and set in motion the divine strategy by which YHWH would call to himself a trustworthy family, one to whom he could commit an inheritance. Abraham gathered his family and investments, both people and flocks, and left Ur to travel to Canaan. On their way, Terah, Abraham's father, died in the city of Haran. Abraham continued the journey, looking for a city whose architect and founder was God (Hebrews 11:8-10). The pathway for YHWH worship had to be built on a different structure than that of Babylonia. He wanted a society that would not be founded the bloated female deities and constellation-oriented priesthood that had reigned with its man-centered perspective for centuries.

The Abrahamic Era

When we begin to read about Abraham in the last part of Genesis 11, we enter this new era in God's dealings with humankind. Noah's flood had come and gone. The newly constituted populations of earth have spread out worldwide and rebuilt themselves into a variety of competing nations. God has set the stage socially, politically, and culturally for the next phase of his salvation history.

In Genesis 12:1-3 YHWH gave this next phase of the future to Abraham. Scripture gives no details about the encounter between YHWH and Abraham that was to be the foundation stone for what we've come to understand as the Abrahamic covenant. God simply spoke to Abraham and outlined for him the divine plan of the ages. Look at the individual promises contained within this covenant:

- I will make you a great nation.
- I will bless you.
- I will make your name great.
- I will make you a blessing to others.
- I will bless those who bless you.
- I will curse those who curse you.
- In you all the peoples of the earth will be blessed.

The final promise declared unequivocally that YHWH would reach all the families on earth through Abraham's faith-response. Those who respond to YHWH, like Abraham, will receive his blessing. Abraham's faith-response and YHWH's progressive revelation about himself provided the cultural context through which God revealed himself as El Elyon, Adonai, and El Shaddai, and eventually the Messiah Christ.

Few people in the Old Testament received the level of revelation given to Abraham. The scope and depth of these promises are staggering. None of the great earthly cultures have developed anything that remotely approaches YHWH's disclosure of his heart and purposes for all humankind. But Abraham's worshiping heart drew the affection of YHWH, who enjoyed relating to Abraham as a "friend" (Isaiah 41:8; James 2:23). Like Abraham, we also become friends of God through faith and worship.

Reflect for a moment on the enormity of this seven-fold promise and on the effect that these covenantal promises have had on you, as the "seed of Abraham." Let your meditation turn into thanksgiving, praise, and worship of the one who put his plans in motion almost 4,000 years ago.

ABRAHAM, THE WORSHIPING PATRIARCH

Abraham's open and exuberant worship of YHWH shows that he was similar in heart attitude to King David. Abraham did not use musical instruments or record poetry-psalms for us, as did David, yet he repeatedly turned to YHWH in gratitude, just like David. Abraham's life was an outflow of obedience that sprang from and led to worship.

Abraham's life was an outflow of obedience that sprang from and led to worship

In the experience with the three visitors in Genesis 18, Abraham fell down and worshiped YHWH as soon as he saw them; some believe this is the first representation of the holy trinity. They confirmed the promise that Sarah would give birth to a son and heir for Abraham. And Abraham worshiped.

Later in Genesis 22, after God had fulfilled the promise of a son, Abraham's faith was tested when he took his son Isaac, in response to YHWH's word, to Mt. Moriah for sacrifice...and for worship. As Abraham took the knife to sacrifice Isaac to YHWH, the Angel of YHWH called to Abraham, telling him not to harm his son. Abraham saw a ram-substitute nearby and offered it to YHWH as sacrifice in place of his son. In response to Isaac's question, Abraham assured him in Genesis 22:8 that "God himself will provide the lamb for the burnt offering, my son."

ALTARS, WORSHIP, AND YIELDEDNESS TO YHWH. Abraham built altars to YHWH from the time he arrived in Canaan. He had traveled southwest from Haran and arrived in the area near Shechem, perhaps 30 miles east of today's Tel Aviv. There, YHWH appeared again to Abraham and reiterated his covenantal promise to give this land to Abraham's descendants (Genesis 12:7). Then Abraham built an altar to YHWH for personal worship and as public witness to the Canaanites who lived in the area.

> **YHWH overcame Abraham's failure with a sweep of justifying grace because he believed that what YHWH said was true**

By faith, Abraham said to the Canaanites that this land was no longer theirs but his, according to YHWH's covenantal word. The worship site bore witness to that promise. Later, Abraham chose this place as a burial site for his wife Sarah. Then Abraham moved a few miles southwest to a site that would become the towns of Bethel and Ai. Again he built an altar to YHWH.

Note God's patterned activity. Each time YHWH spoke or appeared to him, Abraham believed the divine promise and acted on it by worshiping YHWH at an altar he built for that purpose. Abraham gave public testimony to any who asked that he believed YHWH's promises and was committed to their fulfillment. Recall how Abraham twice failed in Egypt (Genesis 12:10-20 and Genesis 20:1-18); yet YHWH overcame that failure with a sweep of justifying grace because Abraham believed that what YHWH said was true.

Chapter Three

EL ELYON, GOD MOST HIGH

The worship of God as El Elyon is first encountered in the Old Testament, in the life of Abraham when he meets Melchizedek, a Canaanite king-priest from the city called Salem. That city would later become Jerusalem. The name Melchizedek means "My king is righteousness," or "king of righteousness, as well as "king of Salem" or "king of peace." In addition to being king, he was also priest of God Most High.

We can only infer Melchizedek's status in the area as priest-king, in keeping with the customs of that time. We must interpret in terms of the people and their cultures, those who first heard these words, namely, those from around 1500 B.C., in Mid-Eastern Palestine. The Genesis writer gives few details, yet at that time many king-priests ruled over cities, city-states, and nations.

Sometimes in larger countries, the king became dominant enough to delegate his priestly functions to lesser officials. Usually, no matter what the priestly leaders stated, the king had the right of veto as well as authority of life and death over the priests. Apparently, in that city of Salem, Melchizedek carried both functions of ruler and priest. But the startling fact is that God had already spoken to Melchizedek previously and revealed this name of El Elyon. Now God was about to use that knowledge of who he is in the life of Abraham.

Since we work with the assumption that the New Testament interprets the Old Testament, we use statements from the book of Hebrews to help us understand this Old Testament leader in

Abraham's time. Melchizedek's identity in Scripture is described in Hebrews 7:3. The writer identifies the king-priest as being "without father or mother, without genealogy, without beginning of days or end of life…like the Son of God he remains a priest forever."

The Genesis writer does not list Melchizedek's parentage or children, birth or death. This is a clear departure from normal Hebrew literary custom. The Hebrews writer uses this absence to characterize Melchizedek as one who is "like the Son of God" in that Jesus does not have a beginning of days or end of life, and remains a priest forever in Father's presence. Melchizedek's priesthood is a type or figure of Christ's priesthood, and his name certainly fits the Son of God as king of peace and righteousness. In addition, as Abraham tithed to Melchizedek, so also we give our tithes and offerings into the hands of Jesus Christ, our great High Priest.

Encountering El Elyon, God Most High

In Genesis 14:1-24, we find some local kings of city-states who reigned as vassals to the greater king Kedorlaomer, king of Elam, a descendent of Noah's second son, Shem. A covenant, in Hebrew *berith*, is the term to represent a working arrangement between a "Great King" and his "Vassal King" for purposes of rulership and administration. The covenant established a permanent bond between these kings, much like a father-son relationship. The Vassal King was to manage and make productive the lesser kingdom on behalf of the Great King. The primary characteristic of this covenant was the establishment of a filial bond between the Great and Vassal Kings. The grants included the following characteristics:

- Unconditional promises from the Great King to the Vassal King
- Unconditional commitment to the Great King by the Vassal King

El Elyon, God Most High

- A self-curse oath on each one in case of non-compliance
- A symbolically enacted ceremony of confirmation
- The sacrifice of animals as witness to the covenant
- Benefits to heirs that continued while their loyalty and service continued

Five vassal kings rebelled against the leadership of Kedorlaomer and so he gathered his four loyal kings for battle against the rebels in the region of the Dead Sea. Kedorlaomer's alliance defeated the five-king group that included the king of Sodom and Gomorrah. They took captives and plundered the cities, taking slaves, including Lot, Abraham's nephew from Sodom. One escaped and reported to Abraham the news of this defeat.

Abraham gathered 318 trained men born of his household and pursued the victorious armies. His nighttime attack routed them and chased them north of Damascus. He recovered all his possessions, as well as his relatives and household—men and women. It is at this point, in Genesis 14:18, that we meet Melchizedek who had left his own city-state to meet this extraordinary man, Abraham, who with only 318 men of his own household defeated and routed the five-king alliance of rebels.

Melchizedek already knew the name of El Elyon and here used it to bless Abraham. Look carefully at the following flow of events: (1) Melchizedek brought out bread and wine, a cultural symbol of peace, of trust and sharing, (2) He blessed Abraham by calling on El Elyon to bless him, (3) He called El Elyon the Creator/Possessor of heaven and earth, (4) He blessed El Elyon the Creator/Possessor of heaven and earth, (5) He blessed El Elyon because El Elyon had delivered Abraham's enemies into his hand, and (6) Abraham gave to Melchizedek a tenth of everything.

Nothing in Scripture has referred to the tithe—yet! We have to wait 400 years for the Mosaic Law to hear God's revealed perspective on tithing, but Abraham responded to the cultural practice of the day and gave this king-priest a tithe of everything.

Many nations of the Mid-East at that time considered their king as a priest and representative of the gods. They gave offerings to their king regularly—not just taxes—for in giving offerings to their king, they were, in fact, giving offerings to their gods. Abraham followed this pattern, recognized Melchizedek as a priest and speaker for his God. Abraham recognized the name El Elyon as another name of YHWH and responded with tithes presented to Melchizedek for the blessing given him.

> **Abraham recognized the name El Elyon as another name of YHWH and responded with tithes to Melchizedek for the blessing**

Now the king of Sodom, who had just approached Abraham to try to negotiate, observed all this interaction between Melchizedek and Abraham, and saw both the tithe given to the king-priest and the people and booty from the battlefield. So he brazenly tried to take YHWH's place by directing Abraham to keep the goods and release his people to him, as though he had a right to both.

Abraham declared that El Elyon is YHWH Elohim, Lord and God Most High. Abraham reinforced his conviction that YHWH was the covenant-giving God. Here, with the king of Sodom challenging him, he made the surprising—indeed, amazing—connection between YHWH Elohim and El Elyon. He lifted his hand toward heaven and swore an oath to YHWH, El Elyon, Creator/Possessor of heaven and earth that he would take nothing of the battlefield booty that represented the possessions of the king of Sodom, "not even a thread or the thong of a san-

El Elyon, God Most High

dal." Abraham would let no one on earth boast that he had made Abraham rich.

Note the incremental release of the Abrahamic covenant, beginning back in Genesis 12. First, YHWH promised the land to Abraham, and when Abraham gave a small piece to Lot, YHWH came to Abraham and reiterated the dimensions of the land he would receive. What Abraham gave away is tiny in comparison to what YHWH bequeathed to him.

Next, YHWH began to make Abraham's name great—great enough to attract both the kings of Sodom and Jerusalem to come and meet him. Then, YHWH promised to bless and enrich Abraham. Abraham had previously come out of Egypt richer than ever before. Now Abraham recovered not only his own possessions but the booty of the battlefield abandoned by the defeated armies. YHWH keeps his covenant promises!

THE NAME EL ELYON

In Hebrew, El Elyon means "highest, exalted God, lifted far above all else." Several characteristics can be identified with this name, El Elyon. When you understand these characteristics, you can worship God with this name and the person of El Elyon, thanking him for who he is and what he does and recognizing his praise-worthy activities in life. The name, El Elyon, Most high God, has the following characteristics, as gleaned from the Biblical contexts in which the name appears.

EL ELYON – MOST HIGH GOD. He reigns as the Universal Sovereign over all. This same Most High God is the sovereign One who rules over all your life and affairs.

EL ELYON – CEO AND ADMINISTRATOR. He selects, installs and sets up all leadership. He establishes greatness and withholds it, including in the case of Satan as morning star in Isaiah 14:12-

14. This is the One who selects, installs and sets up all leadership in your life. He determines exactly who will provide the leadership your life needs.

EL ELYON – POSSESSOR OF ALL HEAVEN AND EARTH. He demonstrates that he alone is the owner of the universe and gives the Kingdom to the saints. The Most High God gives the nations their inheritance and sets up boundaries for the peoples, as stated in Deuteronomy 32:8. This is the same El Elyon who provides for your inheritance and sets up boundaries needed for your protection.

EL ELYON – THE ONE WHO DELIVERS ENEMIES INTO OUR HANDS AND KEEPS FROM DESTRUCTION THOSE WHO KNOW HIM. As Sovereign over all natural forces, his voice resounds; he also shot arrows and scattered David's enemies in Psalm 18:13-14, and delivered him from all his enemies and the hand of Saul in 2 Samuel 22:1. This is the very same One who delivers your enemies into your hands and keeps your from destruction. Let his voice resound and scatter your enemies!

EL ELYON – GREAT HIGH PRIEST, WORTHY OF OUR WORSHIP AND OUR TITHES. See Genesis 14 and Hebrews 7. This is the one who calls you to worship. He is your Great High Priest, the only worthy one. Let his worthiness become your focus for worship and for giving tithes.

WORSHIPING YHWH AS EL ELYON

Worshiping God as El Elyon is an outflow of our awareness and appreciation of who he is. In fact, all worship arises from our own sense of God's worthiness and presence. In worshiping God as El Elyon, let thanksgiving, praise, adoration, and worship arise in the following ways.

THANK EL ELYON. Spread your thanksgiving across the full dimension of his name from Genesis 14, and all other situations where God Most High is mentioned. Let your thanksgiving arise to El Elyon, who according to Daniel, rules over all nations and over the affairs of all mankind. He installs and removes rulers, and protects those thrown into blazing furnaces (Daniel 3:26).

ADORE EL ELYON. Continue in thanksgiving and praise until you sense the stirrings of his presence, the presence of El Elyon. Focus on the characteristics of his name. Declare your love, admiration, adoration, and commitment to El Elyon.

WORSHIP EL ELYON. Worship him for who he is: El Elyon, who fulfills his purposes for you (Psalm 57:2); rest in the shelter of his presence, safe in his refuge and fortress (Psalm 91:1-2); declare with the Psalmist in Psalm 9:2, "I will be glad and rejoice in you; I will sing praise to your Name, O Most High."

WAIT IN SILENCE. Quiet your mind! Tell your soul to rest until his presence comes to you. With the psalmist, wait for his presence to come from the City of God, where the Most High dwells (Psalm 46:4). Wait in silence for El Elyon who also carries the names of Elohim and YHWH Elohim. Let his presence pervade and saturate your mind and soul. The closer his presence, the more silent we become so that we may catch the first breeze of his Spirit, the first scent of his person, the first taste of his goodness, the first sound of his love, the first glimpse of his beauty, his working in our hearts.

> **Tell your soul to rest until his presence comes to you**

MEDITATE ON HIS WORDS AND PURPOSES. Now receive the evidence of his presence, the statements, nuances, perhaps even words that become apparent to you in his presence. His life-giving presence releases our awareness of his word and his purposes. They are faith-giving words, words that console and counsel, words that fortify and challenge.

Chapter Four

ADONAI, SOVEREIGN ONE

No one knows for sure the time span between the end of Genesis 14 and the beginning of 15. The text simply says, "After this." Abraham had shown himself dependable before YHWH, notwithstanding his offense concerning his wife Sarah. Abraham's altar-building custom honored YHWH, both in Abraham's personal worship and especially in a public way by leaving the altars for all who passed that way to see the honor given to YHWH. "After this," YHWH simply visited Abraham in a vision, with no introductory rationale that we know of, and stated abruptly:

- Do not be afraid.
- I am your shield.
- I am giving you a very great reward.

ENCOUNTERING ADONAI: REVEALING GOD'S SOVEREIGN CHARACTER

Adonai has become one of the most-used names of YHWH

In spite of all the covenantal promises, YHWH had discerned Abraham's fear and so came address that fear. YHWH stated that he is Abraham's shield or sovereign, meaning, "I am your Reward and Your King!" The Hebrew noun may be translated either as shield or sovereign. Abram called out, "O Sovereign Lord" (the Hebrew is *adonai morgen*, that is, O Adonai my Sovereign). This name of Adonai later became one of the most used names of YHWH throughout the Scriptures and in Jewish tradition until today. This is seen in the expression, My LORD YHWH, YHWH Adonai.

In speaking of rewards, YHWH wanted to help Abraham keep his balance when it came to kingly riches. Indeed, Abraham lived as a very rich man in those times. But YHWH wanted to remind him that he himself was Abraham's reward, not simply the earthly riches YHWH had given to him. So YHWH came to Abraham in a vision—a reward and riches like no other on earth had ever received before.

Immediately after YHWH's self-revelation, Abraham went to the heart of the issue by addressing YHWH's sovereign character with "O Sovereign Lord." He reminded YHWH that although he had given him all these promises, Abraham had no heir to receive these promises after he died. In fact, Abraham had thought about following the cultural pattern by adopting his male servant, Eliezer, and bequeathing his entire estate to him.

YHWH then intervened to quiet Abraham's fears by declaring his own sovereign solution, "... a son coming from your own body will be your heir!" Paul says in Romans 4:20 that Abraham did not waver through unbelief in the face of YHWH's extraordinary promise. Abraham's response to YHWH's words became a foundation stone in New Testament teaching: "Abraham believed YHWH and he credited it to him as righteousness" (Genesis 15:6).

Abraham was fully persuaded that GOD had the power to do what he promised. Hebrews 11:11 says, "By faith Abraham, even though he was past age...was enabled to become a father because he considered him faithful who had made the promise." After giving the promise to Abraham, YHWH took him outside the tent and told him to look up at the starry heavens. If Abraham

ADONAI, SOVEREIGN ONE

could count the stars of heaven, then he could count the number of descendants that YHWH would give him.

Immediately YHWH continued the dialogue by reiterating the promise of Genesis 12:1-3 and 13:14-17, that YHWH brought Abraham out of Ur of the Chaldeans in order to give him this land for his possession. In one moment, out of a deep filial bond, YHWH forgave all his sins, and in the next reassured Abraham that he would possess the land where he was standing. Abraham again asked the "how" questions, not the "if" question. He wanted to know how YHWH would carry this out, not if he would carry it out.

Abraham's faith-response to YHWH's promises earned him the title, "father of the faithful," that is, all those that are full of faith. Paul used this verse in Galatians and Romans to show that believers today are saved just like Abraham—we are all justified by faith.

THE CEREMONY THAT VALIDATES THE PROMISE. In the structures of Mid-Eastern covenants, there is always some sort of ceremony that both parties embrace to demonstrate that the covenantal promises are in force and operative. Just before the ceremony, Abraham fell asleep and YHWH spoke to him in the midst of a "thick and dreadful darkness." YHWH stated that his descendants would be enslaved in a foreign land for 400 years, after which YHWH would bring them forth to possess this land, a territory that stretched from the Euphrates to the Nile. Abraham would not see this, but his descendants would fulfill it.

In Genesis 15:9, YHWH told Abraham what animals to acquire for the ceremony. Abraham sacrificed them, cutting them in two and laying half of each animal on one side of a trail and the other half on the other side, leaving a path down the middle. Now in the ceremony, verses 10-21, YHWH Adonai came in a "smoking firepot" with a blazing torch and passed down the trail between the pieces. No one is quite sure just what the Hebrew words are trying to convey here. But the custom in covenant-making provided that each official involved, such as the Great King with his Vassal King, must walk down that pathway between the animals. Each participant was fully cognizant that the slaughtered animals were a picture of what would happen to them if they broke the covenant.

YHWH came to earth at this point and walked down that pathway to validate for Abraham the covenantal promises. Apparently, with the smoking firepot and blazing torch, YHWH took full responsibility to effect this covenantal promise, since the text does not mention that Abraham passed between the slaughtered animals. He was still sleeping, caught in the awesome "thick and dreadful darkness."

> **YHWH set his love on Abraham and the he enveloped Abraham in his love, the more Abraham responded in faith**

The promises were now in force and both parties had agreed to fulfill all the stipulations that accompanied the promises. YHWH's presence calls to mind a similar ceremony at Calvary when Jesus, alone, walked down a similar pathway that led to the cross. He became the guarantor of the covenant of forgiveness, as though he were the sinner who deserved to die. Jesus of Nazareth, just like ancient YHWH, took upon himself the full responsibility of our sin, and by walking down that pathway, obligated himself to an ignoble death for mankind's broken covenant, even as YHWH showed His covenant through the slaughtered animals of Abraham's day. Therein was the promise sealed forever.

Pause and consider the enormity of this scenario: the God of heaven and earth descended in person, spoke with Abraham, and initiated and confirmed his own promises with Abraham.

YHWH had set his love on Abraham and the more he enveloped Abraham in his love, the more Abraham responded in faith. Adonai enjoyed Abraham so much that Adonai called him his friend.

THE NAME ADONAI

Think about the enormity and gravity of YHWH's promises to Abraham, for they are part of your inheritance in Christ Jesus, who is the Offspring of Abraham (Galatians 3:16-19). Abraham had a problem with fear that YHWH came to address. Abraham was doubtless surprised that YHWH not only reassured him, but went on to restate the covenant promises of Genesis 12 and then engage a ceremony to confirm the covenant.

The name Adonai means "Lord" in Hebrew and is translated as the well-known Greek term *kupios* in Hebrew-Greek translations. We understand the meaning of the term from its multiple contexts in the Old Testament. As you read over Genesis 15, notice that this is the name Abraham used for YHWH in their conversation. Here Abram showed the posture of his heart towards YHWH by calling him Adonai. The characteristics reflected through this name in various scriptural contexts show us who Adonai is in terms of what he does and how he relates to people.

In addition to references to YHWH, the name Adonai was used for government officials (lord, master), as in Genesis 42:10 where Joseph's brothers address him as "Adonai," sovereign king, without recognizing him as their brother. King Abimelech also uses the term to refer to God when he had taken Abraham's wife into his harem, thinking she was his sister, not wife. Elohim came to him in a dream and terrified him. Abimelech responded and recognized him as, "Adonai, Lord…" (Genesis 20:4).

YHWH ADONAI – GOD WHO REWARDS WHOSE WHO OBEY HIM. In Genesis 13:14-15, God first promised Abraham a great inheritance of land and offspring as numerous as the dust of the earth. As Adonai, in Genesis 15, he speaks directly to Abraham and confirms his covenant word to provide for him. This same Adonai will provide "all your needs according to the riches of his glory in Christ Jesus (Philippians 4:19).

ADONAI – GOD WHO JUSTIFIES SINNERS. In Genesis 15:6, we see Abraham's faith-response to Adonai's promises: "He believed the Lord, and he credited it to him as righteousness." Adonai brings forth righteousness because it is his nature. The Sovereign Lord will make righteousness and praise to spring up before all nations (Isaiah 61:11). This same Adonai justifies you through the blood of Jesus and waits to hear and see your faith response in his son Jesus.

ADONAI – GOD WHO GUARANTEES ALL PROMISES WITH HIS OWN LIFE. Adonai walked between the rows of slaughtered animals to validate the covenant he initiated with Abraham (Genesis 15:10-22). Adonai makes and keeps promises. He is the true promise-maker and promise-keeper. He kept every promise made to Abraham. And he will keep every promise he has made to you. Jesus is the guarantee by his blood shed on the cross.

ADONAI – GOD WHO IS SOVEREIGN LORD OVER ALL. Adonai is Sovereign Lord. His sovereignty arched over all aspects of Abraham's life, present and future. Trust was his foundation. In Moses' life, he pled with Adonai YHWH to let him cross the Jordan into the Promised Land instead of just seeing it (Deuteronomy 3:23). But in his sovereignty, Adonai denied the request and his decisions are final and to be trusted. This same Adonai is sovereign over all the affairs of your life today and all the days to come: Adonai, Sovereign, trustworthy Father.

ADONAI – GOD WHO PROTECTS ALL HIS SERVANTS. Adonai protected Abraham in each life encounter. Joshua also worshiped before Adonai, the one who came as "commander of the army of the LORD" (Joshua 5:14). Gideon also received a guarantee from

Adonai that together they would strike down the enemy (Judges 6:16, 22). He commands every force that we encounter and protects and provides for each life encounter.

Worshiping YHWH as Adonai

Reflect on YHWH Adonai. The Great God of the universe stepped into his own creation and spoke in vision form to his servant Abraham. YHWH Adonai was under no legal or moral compulsion to make contact with earth's perverted and self-centered population. But the constraints of his own nature, his overall goal of establishing fellowship with humankind, his impassioned desire to embrace his lost family all combined to move YHWH Adonai to enter human history about 2000 B.C. to relate with Abraham.

The Great God of the universe intruded into his own creation, appeared as a smoking firepot with a blazing torch, and confirmed the covenant he had come to celebrate with Abraham. The Great God of the universe provided an answer to Abraham's dilemma: Abraham certainly believed and trusted Adonai but had no idea just how all these promises could happen in his lifetime. So Adonai bent the laws of nature to his own will: he promised that Abraham would have a son of his own by Sarah, even though both were past the child-bearing time of life.

> **As Abraham developed a life-attitude of faith he gazed at the heart of the triune God**

Meditate on who Adonai is and all he has done. Note especially these actions by YHWH Adonai:

- YHWH Adonai wiped clear Abraham's sin because he believed YHWH'S word. This is the meaning of the word "justify."
- Just as YHWH walked down that path between the animals, so also YHWH-Jesus walked down the same path at the cross for you.
- Adonai gave this vision to Abraham to set motive and purpose before Abraham, to covenant with and give Abraham a solid base for relating with him. Abraham developed this life attitude of faith, a faith that gazes steadily at Adonai YHWH, and without realizing it, he gazed at the heart of the Triune God.

RESPOND with your praise to YHWH Adonai's assertion that he is your shield and reward. Spend time in thanksgiving and praise of YHWH who is Adonai, the One who justifies sinners, and guarantees all promises with his own life.

WORSHIP AND ADORE YHWH Adonai. Enter into the silence of Adonai's presence, as did Abraham. Perhaps he will give you a vision-word that maps out the future as you walk in his Kingdom. Worship him as Adonai, Sovereign, Wrap-around Shield, the One Who Clears Guilt of those who believe his words. Worship Adonai your Protector, your Guarantor, your Promise Maker and Promise Keeper, the Only One Who Can Bring forth righteousness here on earth. Worship him for his worthiness as Adonai.

Chapter Five

EL SHADDAI, GOD ALMIGHTY

At 75 years of age Abraham left Haran for Palestine, thinking that his servant Eliezor would be his heir. Then, at 86, he had a son, Ishmael, by his concubine Hagar (Genesis 16). But YHWH made it clear to Abraham that he did not consider Ishmael the fulfillment or heir of the promise (Genesis 15:4) but that Abraham would have a son from his own body. Now at 99 years of age YHWH again appeared to Abraham and identified himself as El Shaddai, a God-Name not previously known, a name that signifies invincible power and provision.

ENCOUNTERING EL SHADDAI

In Genesis 17:1-2, YHWH El Shaddai told Abraham that he had appeared to him to confirm the covenant already given in chapters 12 and 15. Genesis 12 gave the overview of YHWH's covenant promises and blessings. In Genesis 15 YHWH emphasized the promise of descendants and the land. Here in Genesis 17, YHWH focused on the numbers of peoples and nations that Abraham would father and influence. He told him "I am God Almighty; walk before me and be blameless. I will confirm my covenant between me and you and will greatly increase your numbers." Nine times in this passage YHWH mentions that the covenant is his: he initiates it, he confirms it, and he establishes and fulfills it. This statement illustrates the quality of

> **The covenant is YHWH's: he initiates, confirms, establishes and fulfills it**

God's covenants: he makes the arrangement and offers it freely to the ones he chooses.

At this juncture Abraham fell face down, a strong worship response that declared his committed faith and obedience. El Shaddai then expanded and described the previously unreleased details of the covenant. The covenantal terms recorded in Genesis 17:1-8 are:

- El Shaddai made Abraham a father of many nations.
- El Shaddai changed Abram's name from "exalted father," to Abraham, "father of many."
- El Shaddai promised to make Abraham very fruitful.
- El Shaddai promised to make Abraham the progenitor of many nations and kings.
- El Shaddai established his covenant as an everlasting covenant between himself and Abraham with his descendants for generations to come.
- El Shaddai declared himself to be God, the YHWH Elohim of Abraham and the Lord God of his descendants.
- El Shaddai vowed to give the entire land of Canaan as an everlasting possession to Abraham and his descendants.

> **YHWH looks for responses that fully reflect the faith Abraham carried in his heart**

THE CEREMONY THAT VALIDATED THIS COVENANT. YHWH El Shaddai continued his explanation to Abraham in 17: 9-14. He wanted Abraham and his descendants to keep this covenant for generations to come. YHWH was looking for a response that fully reflected the faith Abraham carried in his heart. Paul calls it, "the obedience that comes from faith" (Romans 1:5). That is the worship lifestyle that pleases GOD.

As a way of validating this covenant, El Shaddai introduced a new component. He wanted every male to be circumcised then and in all generations to come. By this ceremonial act of circumcision, this act of worship, YHWH placed a mark on the body of every male showing that he belonged to El Shaddai. This was a commitment to perpetual obedience to his covenant.

Notice that by circumcision, every male of Israel declared in a very personal and irrevocable way that his own power to procreate was dedicated to YHWH. Circumcision marked all covenanted males in the dedication of their sexual life and offspring to YHWH El Shaddai. Circumcision consecrated the male child to YHWH alone. Circumcision was an act of worship for an Israelite father in dedication of his male children and their descendants to YHWH. Circumcision resembles an oath that could be expressed as: "If I am not loyal in faith and obedience to my LORD, may the LORD cut me off, as well as my descendants."

This validation ceremony focused on the dedication of each male, especially in his sexual activity, to YHWH El Shaddai. Here, YHWH El Shaddai also reconfirms Abraham's innumerable descendants and pushes the continuance of this covenant into the indefinite future. Again YHWH reassured Abraham that the whole land of Canaan was his as an everlasting possession.

El Shaddai also covered Sarah in the covenant. In Genesis 17:15-16, YHWH El Shaddai involved Sarah in his dealings with Abraham. He changed her name from Sarai to Sarah. Both names cover the idea of "princess," but the latter name Sarah includes a series of personal promises to her:

- YHWH El Shaddai will bless her.
- YHWH El Shaddai will give a son to Abraham through Sarah.
- YHWH El Shaddai will make her the mother of nations.

- YHWH El Shaddai will cause kings to come from her body.

Abraham responded by falling down and laughing to himself about the apparent impossibility of his wife getting pregnant since she was 90 years of age. He suggested to YHWH El Shaddai that he might better consider Ishmael as the bearer of the covenantal promises. But YHWH ignored the suggestion and reinforced his own oath that Sarah would bear a son whom they were to name Isaac, which means "laughter." Later, in response to YHWH's appearance near the great trees of Mamre when the three visitors came to initiate the promise (Genesis 18:12), Sarah took her turn at laughing in response to God's promise. But, forever Sarah stands as the "free woman" whose son came by YHWH's promise (Genesis 21). All devious, self-seeking activities were now forgiven. Sarah stands for the new covenant validated at Mt. Calvary in Jerusalem (Galatians 4:24-26).

And then to complete the promise, thirteen years after YHWH's promise to Abraham and Sarah, they were given their son Isaac whom Abraham circumcised. Thereby YHWH announced the Gospel in advance through Abraham that he would justify the Gentiles by faith (see Galatians 3:8). They had obeyed YHWH and sent Hagar out of their household so that YHWH could give her and her son another set of promises.

Abraham walked in the reality of the triune God and because of his faith response to YHWH he experienced his revelatory activity through the names El Elyon, Adonai, and El Shaddai.

The statements of promise to Abraham and Sarah revealed the first explanation of God's Name, El Shaddai. The Hebrew word itself speaks of omnipotent power and abundance. El Shaddai is the One who abounds and shares that abundance. The terms of the covenant describe that power and its unimaginable abundance in terms of people, leaders and real estate. No wonder Abraham fell down twice (Genesis 17: 3 and 17:17)!

The name El Shaddai means something like, "the Mountain One," signifying invincible power, to be burly or powerful. But it also carries the sense of enormous abundance. The covenant of Genesis 17 demonstrated that power with its unimaginable abundance, in terms of descendants, kings and rulers, and tracts of land.

But one more stipulation appeared in Genesis 17:1, never seen before. In contrast to YHWH'S other encounters with Abraham, YHWH here explained that his intentions for Abraham were to be perfect, that is, mature or whole. The NIV uses the term "blameless," that is, one who is without reproach or, the one against whom no one can point a finger for unresolved offenses. YHWH wanted Abraham to be a man of integrity. The Bible is honest about Abraham's failings, but apparently, Abraham's faith brought justifying grace from YHWH.

Now the time had arrived for YHWH to begin to insist on consistent living before him. Abraham's faith-response to YHWH should begin to carry into Abraham's lifestyle the character of the one in whom Abraham trusted. YHWH wanted Abraham to realize that he would fulfill all terms of his covenant, with its many promises, but he wanted Abraham to live before his contemporaries with the same character that YHWH had displayed to him all his days on earth.

EL SHADDAI – HE IS THE MULTIGENERATIONAL GOD AND ONE WHO BLESSES. His blessing to Abraham and Sarah was rich and deep and eternal. He did this to show himself great and to fulfill his purposes on earth. In Genesis 35:11, El Shaddai spoke to Jacob using the same name he introduced to Abraham, and assured Jacob that the covenant extended to him and his coming generations. This same El Shaddai extends his blessing to you through Jesus in your pursuit of his name.

EL SHADDAI – HE IS GOD WHO CALLS BELIEVERS TO BE BLAMELESS. He expects those who trust him to live like he does in attitude and lifestyle. Job 5:16 and 6:4 show how believers are disciplined by El Shaddai and may unknowingly attribute their suffering and problems to him. But he calls us to holy living because he is holy. 2 Corinthians 6:17 refers to Isaiah 52:11, exhorting God's people to separate themselves from sin and he will be their father and they will be his sons and daughters. This El Shaddai wants you to be conformed to the image of his dear son Jesus.

EL SHADDAI - HE HAS INVINCIBLE POWER. El Shaddai brings righteousness to bear and destruction upon disobedient nations (Isaiah 13:6 and Revelation 19:15). His power breaks the power of the enemy. This El Shaddai will break the power of the enemy in your life as well.

EL SHADDAI – HE HAS ENORMOUS ABUNDANCE. El Shaddai promised to bless Jacob's sons with blessings of heaven above and from the deep that lies below (Genesis 49:25-26). This is the one who has many good things for you, his people (Psalm 103)

EL SHADDAI – HE CALLS US TO LAY DOWN ALL WE HOLD DEAR IN THIS LIFE. Whereby we might be called by the name of the All-Powerful One. This included the price of circumcision that Abraham, his male household, and all succeeding male Jews have paid so that their family-nation might be set-apart to YHWH El Shaddai (Genesis 17:1-14). This is the one who calls you to offer him all you hold dear to receive "every spiritual blessing in Christ" (Ephesians 1:17).

El Shaddai, God Almighty

Worshiping YHWH as El Shaddai

GIVE THANKS TO EL SHADDAI. Give him thanks that he blesses and makes you a blessing. He enriches you so you can enrich others. He increases you so you can bring increase to others. He multiplies the work of your hands and supplies all resources to fulfill his purposes. And give thanks that he goes to great length to conform you to his image.

PRAISE EL SHADDAI. Give El Shaddai praise, for he is the multigenerational God, the God of Abraham, the God of Isaac, and the God of Jacob. He is your God and the God of your descendants after you.

- Give praise to El Shaddai, for he is ultimately responsible for the difficulties that come into your life. But he controls them that we, like Abraham, might come to maturity in lifestyle.
- Give praise to El Shaddai, for he is the one who supervises nations, including your nation, and their rulers, calling them to account for disobedience and blessing them for obedience.
- Give praise to El Shaddai, for his enormous blessing showered from heaven on you from your earliest remembrances of him, even long before you yielded to him.
- Give praise to El Shaddai, for his filial relationship and fatherly call to you to maintain a lifestyle that brings honor to his name and brings you close to him.
- Give praise to El Shaddai, who calls you to lay down to him your dearest possessions and peoples, as did Abraham, to be circumcised in heart and carry the mark in your life that identifies you as his own.
- Give praise to El Shaddai, for he is the one who brings blessings into your life, even as he brought unimaginable blessings into Abraham and Sarah's life.

WORSHIP AND ADORE EL SHADDAI. Bow in silence before YHWH El Shaddai, the One who calls you to holy living because he himself is holy. He calls you to a life of obedience as demonstration of your faith-love towards him. Worship and adore the one who is worthy.

BOW IN SILENCE. Bow in silence before him who calls us to lay down everything we hold dear in this life that he might become the all-powerful one in your lives—as did Abraham when he offered up Isaac in full faith that YHWH would raise him from the dead. Bow in silence before him who also carries the name: THE ETERNAL ONE. And in the silence may his Spirit touch your spirit!

WAIT FOR HIM TO SHARE HIS HEART AND WORD. Listen for the voice of El Shaddai in your quietness. Let him expand your awareness of himself and all the names that God revealed during Abraham's walk here on earth: El Elyon, Adonai, and El Shaddai.

Section Three

Worshiping YHWH in the Mosaic Era

At this next point in revelation history, we step into the era dominated by God's dealings with Moses. The self-revealing activities of the God of Abraham, YHWH Adonai El Shaddai, were about to move into a greatly enlarged sphere. Up to now YHWH worked with individuals and families, revealing himself by name and instructing them how to handle life within his purposes. Both Noah and Abraham received the covenant from YHWH that projected unimaginable blessings upon future believers and nations.

How profoundly different the man Moses! He came into life as a child with Hebrew parents that lived as slaves under Pharaoh, the most powerful ruler on earth. By miraculous intervention, Moses was planted as an adopted son in Pharaoh's household. Pharaoh's daughter and royal court brought him up as potential heir to Pharaoh's throne. They trained him in languages and diplomacy, sciences and literature, military affairs and administration. How grieved Pharaoh must have felt when this "ascending star" betrayed him and his nation by killing an Egyptian official. Banished from Egypt, Moses was expelled to the Sinai wilderness.

Such are the ways of YHWH Elohim, who is El Elyon, Most High God, and Adonai, Sovereign Lord, and El Shaddai, God Almighty. The mission YHWH had for Moses differed remarkably from that of Abraham. From here on, YWHW would work with his people as a nation.

Moses, in his role as leader of this new nation, presided at the giving of YHWH's Law at Mt. Sinai, the Law that called all humanity into account before the Living God (Romans 3:19). He also presided at the dissolution of the Egyptian Empire, Pharaoh's jewel and embodiment of eternal life. Like Daniel, Moses revealed and mediated the successive blows that broke the glory, power and wisdom of a dominant society.

In Abraham's day, God showed himself as the Most High God, Sovereign Lord and God Almighty. Notice the emphasis on his absoluteness, his position without rivals, and his covenants. Now we are about to see his irresistible power in human society and his compassionate approach to people. God trained Moses to carry his revelation of authority to human society by the right of his unique existence, as surely as he trained Abraham to disclose his sovereignty and justification.

When looking back at what YHWH had already done to introduce his name to the nation that had become Israel, YHWH's "chosen," the content of the divine name has grown fuller and more complete. But now we see a 400-year hiatus in Egypt during which YHWH transformed Abraham's descendants from a family of 70 adults into some two million men, women and children. Admittedly, they are a mass of slaves, nurtured in the Egyptian language, culture, and god-system, but with a living tradition of YHWH-encounters from the days of Abraham.

At this point in revelation history, YHWH gives to Moses the full content of his name YHWH. All the details of previous encounters of YHWH as Elohim, YHWH Elohim, El Elyon, Adonai and El Shaddai, found their way into the Torah, the teaching of YHWH about himself and his chosen nation, Israel. These encounters are now permanently inscribed in the Law of Moses.

From this point on, about 1450 BC, YHWH brings his presence directly into the camp of Israel. He intended to live among people, his purpose since the human failure in the Garden. As God's people travel through the wilderness, he is directly accessible only to those of Aaron's blood line, the priests. Yet the people of Israel get to watch YHWH's presence accompanying them daily as a cloud and each night as a column of fire.

YHWH is compassionate in his jealousy for his people's affections

YHWH IS COMPASSIONATE IN HIS JEALOUSY FOR HIS PEOPLE'S AFFECTIONS. During Israel's wanderings, YHWH shared another name with Moses, the name of Quannah. Quannah, simply means "jealous." YHWH was and still is jealous for the hearts of his people, as he told Moses in Exodus 34:14. YHWH instructed Moses that they were to be diligent in dealing with the native populations within the territory YHWH gave to Israel. God's people were never to make a treaty with those tribal groups. More than that, Moses insisted that the Israelites break down, smash, and cut down all idols and worship paraphernalia of the local peoples, especially the local female deities like Asherah, lest they become a snare to Israel. The reason for this command is that the LORD YHWH, whose name is Quannah, or Jealous is "a jealous God."

In Deuteronomy 4:24 and 6:15, we see YHWH's jealousy like a consuming fire. Such jealousy bespeaks a depth of love and concern unknown on earth among any god-system. The phrase "consuming fire" describes what is meant by jealous. When YHWH is jealous, he is also angry at those who are making him jealous with worthless idols (Deuteronomy 32:21). All god-systems devised by mortals build on an exchange principle: "I will worship this god if that god will do something for me." By contrast, YHWH set out to build a national mindset that lifted worship to him because he is worthy of that worship. No other culture on earth had a God both compassionate and jealous.

YHWH's name as Jealous occurs nowhere else in the Scriptures with the same emphasis. Yet many times in Scripture we see it used as an adjective to describe YHWH. In the giving of the second commandment, Exodus 20:5, YHWH said of himself that "I, the Lord your God, am a jealous God."

Later, in a covenantal ceremony in Joshua's farewell address to Israel (Joshua 24:19), he reminds the people that they will not be able to serve the LORD YHWH without a deep and persistent commitment to him, for YHWH is a holy God and a jealous God. So the jealousy attributed to YHWH includes the anger of wrath along with the holiness that brings to the offenders a consuming fire. The exclusivity of YHWH to his people is nowhere else so emphasized as in the use of this name, "Quannah" or Jealous.

Chapter Six

THE GREAT I AM

Close to four hundred years have passed since YHWH, Adonai, El Elyon, El Shaddai made promises and swore covenant with Abraham in Genesis 13, 15 and 17. YHWH's self-revealing activities are about to move into a greatly enlarged sphere.

Incredibly, YHWH next engaged his own revealed purpose of redeeming a nation for himself rather than just individuals or families. He took on the nation that ruled supreme in the Mid-Eastern world, a nation that boasted several thousand years of unbroken divine leadership through their god-incarnate pharaohs. YHWH intended to open the way for an entire nation to approach him in worship. He was about to release the depths of his most personal name, YHWH! Up until now, he is YHWH Elohim, the God of relationship. Now he wants to add another dimension to his Name of YHWH and reveal himself as the Great I AM.

YHWH heard the suffering of his people and remembered his covenant with Abraham, Isaac and Jacob

God so arranged the lives of Moses' and Pharaoh's family that Moses became an orphan, rescued by Pharaoh's daughter, brought up in the royal court of Egypt with all the privileges of Pharaoh's own children. Moses struggled with his heritage, probably imparted first through his own mother and then through Pharaoh's daughter. With inappropriate and self-righteous leadership, he then killed an Egyptian who beat a fellow Hebrew. He fled the death sentence imposed by Pharaoh, and took haven in Midian, the eastern side of today's Persian Gulf. He rescued the daughters of the priest of Midian from harsh shepherds, stayed with the priest's family and eventually married one of the daughters, Zipporah. Moses tended sheep in the Midian wilderness, while Israel groaned in increasingly grievous slavery under Egyptian taskmasters. But YHWH heard their suffering and remembered his covenant with Abraham, Isaac, and Jacob, the ancestors of Moses.

Encountering YHWH, the Great I Am

One day while shepherding in Midian, in the vicinity of Mt. Sinai, the Angel of YHWH appeared in the flames of an unconsumed burning bush. Moses saw the unusual happening and moved closer to inspect it. YHWH called Moses by name, instructed him to take off his sandals for it was holy ground on which he stood. Next he proceeded to disclose his name as "the Elohim of your father, the Elohim of Abraham, the Elohim of Isaac and the Elohim of Jacob" (Exodus 3:6). God used the name Elohim because at the time of Moses' forefathers—Abraham, Isaac and Jacob—the meaning of the name YHWH had not yet been fully revealed.

> **The self-revelation of YHWH at Sinai is the most important intrusion of God into human affairs since the flood**

There in the encounter at the bush, YHWH disclosed his heart to Moses, his deep concern for the suffering of his people, and his call on Moses' life to lead his people from Egypt to the promised land. To validate himself before the people of Israel, Moses requested the name of the One speaking to him. Without hesitation, Elohim said to Moses, "I AM WHO I AM is the One sending you to Israel." He accentuated it by authorizing Moses to tell the people of Israel, "I AM has sent me to you" (Exodus 3:14). YHWH Elohim, the God of their ancestors—Abraham, Isaac and Jacob—was sending Moses to them, and said, "This is my name forever, the name by which I am to be remembered from generation to generation" (Exodus 3:15).

This self-revelation by YHWH constitutes the most important and penetrating intrusion of God into human affairs on earth since the flood. In the face of intolerable and suffocating self-centeredness, God had brought judgment to earth's inhabitants through the flood. But on Mt. Sinai—in the brilliance of a burning and unconsumed bush—YHWH revealed his compassion and jealous passion for Israel. In the following months, the fierceness of his love consumed the entire Egyptian nation. The message remains clear to this day: Let no one stand between YHWH and his chosen people Israel.

YHWH Versus Pharaoh. We are about to watch the dismantling of an entire nation—its agriculture, military might, vaulted learning and architecture, its entire god-system, and its leadership—all would collapse at the feet of YHWH during this extended confrontation. Pharaoh would face this insistent refrain, "Let my people go that they may worship me!" In his refusal, Pharaoh would also face the dissolution of his leadership, a leadership whose foundation extended back thousands of years. With each plague, over and over came this clear command of YHWH: "Let my people go that they may worship me."

After six powerful plagues, just before the plague of hail of his Presence, YHWH told Moses to tell Pharaoh, that "I have raised you up for this very purpose, that I might show you my power and that my name might be proclaimed in all the earth" (Exodus 9:16). Pharaoh's reaction to YHWH was in effect, "These people belong to me, not you. I will not let them go to worship you!" So started the hammering blows of successive plagues and disasters all over Egypt. Pharaoh had to be convinced that YHWH was the person he claimed to be.

In the end, Pharaoh's final act of defiance came in the face of a nation that lay in ruins, with its posterity and national life devastated. Not heeding the forces that had just been unleashed against him, he sent his army, his ultimate basis of power, in a pursuit that ended in a watery grave under the Red Sea. YHWH's call to release his people provoked in Pharaoh an unyielding belligerent reaction. Pharaoh, trapped in his anger, resentment, and pride, lost everything that mattered.

Israel meanwhile, having watched as every firstborn in Egypt—human or animal—died at midnight, while the Israelite children slept in peace, protected by the blood of the lamb over each doorpost. Israel embraced the Passover Feast and heard the command to leave Egypt to worship YHWH. Israel, an impoverished slave-nation for 400 years, suddenly found itself carrying the wealth of Egypt out across the Red Sea and into that terrible desert where the awesome holiness of YHWH awaited them at Mt. Sinai.

WORSHIP: THE PURPOSE OF THE EXODUS FROM EGYPT. Notice the sequence of events leading up to the release of YHWH's purpose. Note especially that YHWH always makes the first move to attract our attention to him.

- YHWH initiated his self-disclosure by igniting a bush that burned with his presence that remained unconsumed and by calling out to Moses to come near, but to respect his holiness.
- YHWH openly disclosed the meaning of his most personal name to Moses.
- **When Moses worshiped**, YHWH commissioned Moses to demand the release of his people from Pharaoh.

- YHWH demanded that Pharaoh release his people **so that they may worship him.**
- Pharaoh refused to worship YHWH; this refusal brought upon Egypt utter and complete destruction.
- YHWH brought his people forth to worship him!

Everything else was secondary to worship, including the rescue from bondage and the formation of a nation. YHWH was determined to create from an idol-worshiping slave rabble a covenant nation characterized by order, prosperity, and YHWH-worship who would serve as a public example and display before Gentile nations of YHWH's goodness and excellence.

> **The central issue of the exodus was worship; everything else was secondary**

The conflict that YHWH precipitated with Egypt parallels the encounter of Jesus of Nazareth with Satan, god of this world system, over the issue of worship. Jesus has set "free those who all their lives were held in slavery" (Hebrews 2:15). We are set free that we may worship him. The goal of Jesus' saving activity is worship. He brought us out of enslavement to our gods, the all-encompassing idols of the world system, to worship the Living YHWH.

THE NAME YHWH, I AM WHO I AM

The name, I AM WHO I AM, may also be translated, I WILL BE WHO I WILL BE. His name is the simple Hebrew verb "to be," present tense, and is also transliterated *ehyeh*, that is the Hebrew word rendered in English letters for I AM: YHWH is simply translated as "He is," the One who is, the One who exists and has always existed. YHWH is the reason for the existence of all things besides himself. In this simple but profound name, we find the summation of all that exists in this person YHWH.

There is a great breadth of meaning inherent in this name, YHWH. At the experience of the Burning Bush, the LORD told Moses that "YHWH" is his Name and always has been and always will be—for a thousand generations and for all eternity! He is the reason for your existence.

YHWH I AM– EXISTS WITH NO LIMITS. The semantic inferences of the name YHWH challenge the mind and imagination, for God chooses the verb "to be" as a vehicle for carrying the breadth and depth of his own person. It is too confining to speak of "as high as the heavens," or "the depths of the sea." It is still too confining to speak of "the edges of the universe." For YHWH is the very ground and reason for all existence. He exists outside this universe where he placed us and he steps into his own universe to display the fullness of his person to any who will listen for him.

YHWH, the one who exists in and of himself, has no limits as mankind defines limits. He lives, moves and works in terms of the limits within his own person, the limits as revealed later in Exodus 34:6-7 when he declares to Moses the fullness of his own YHWH name. He openly showed Moses the meaning of his own most personal name. Then he commissioned Moses to demand from Pharaoh the release of his people to worship him. YHWH always makes the first move. He alone has that right and power in your life, with no limits.

YHWH I AM – HAS ABSOLUTE AND FINAL AUTHORITY OVER ALL THAT EXISTS. The name YHWH carries such absolute and final authority over all that exists in heaven and on earth that Moses would use it almost as a weapon in all confrontations with Pharaoh. When YHWH commanded Pharaoh to release his people, Pharaoh resisted because he thought that the Israelites were his. Pharaoh had no idea the dimensions of the person YHWH. But he learned that YHWH has the right and authority, and the power to make it happen, to dictate the future of any nation on earth, and to call individuals or kings into account before him. YHWH has this final authority in your life.

YHWH I AM – IS COMPLETELY WITHIN HIS INHERENT RIGHTS TO DO WHAT'S IN HIS HEART. When YHWH chose Israel—just because he chose Israel—to be his own special people, he is within his rights. Later when YHWH directed Moses to destroy and dispossess nations, Canaanites, or others, he is completely within his inherent rights. And he is within his rights to do whatever is in his heart for you today.

YHWH I AM – IS PASSIONATE IN HIS LOVE-CARE AND INTERVENES ON BEHALF OF HIS PEOPLE. YHWH, passionate for his people, reached out to embrace Israel because he wanted a worshiping nation who would fellowship with him, freely and lovingly. We find perhaps the most poignant expression of YHWH's love care for Israel in Hosea's story of an unfaithful wife and the faithful husband as an example of God's faithful, persistent love. YHWH related to Israel in love, in that he has betrothed himself to Israel forever (Hosea 2:19). He wants to have mercy on Israel, rather than receive more sacrifices from Israel (Hosea 6:6). YHWH wants Israel to reap the fruit of unfailing love (Hosea 10:12). And in the midst of Israel's sin, YHWH calls her again to himself; he will show his love again, to the one called "not loved," and "not my people" (Hosea 2:23), and they will say, "You are my God." Let your heart, the not-loved but now loved, declare, "You are my God."

> **Let your heart, the not-loved-but-now-loved, declare, "You are my God"**

YHWH I AM - IS HOLY AND CALLS US TO WORSHIP HIM. The name YHWH carries holiness. That is, the essence of YHWH's person. Leviticus 11:44 exhorts us, "You shall be holy because I am holy." YHWH's holiness, or essence, wherever it alights, purges and heals whatever surrounds it—purges all that resists him and heals all who receive him. Revelation 4: 8 sums it up: "Holy, Holy, Holy is the Lord God Almighty, who was and is and is to come. "Consecrate yourself and be holy because I AM is holy. Worship the Lord God Almighty with all your heart.

WORSHIPING GOD AS YHWH, THE GREAT I AM

As you prepare for worship, remember this above everything else: He is compassionate in his jealousy and passionate in his love care. The fierceness of his holiness cleanses everything before, around, or near it. The YHWH name has no imitations, no rivals, no limits.

THANK YHWH. Reflect on the sequence of events leading up to the full self-revelation and encounter with the gods of that age. Use this as a starting point for approaching YHWH. Then reflect on the events leading up to his encounter with the gods of this age in your life, and how his passion for you has set you free to worship him and be a demonstration of his passionate love. As you give thanks and praise YHWH, other items will arise in your mind and spirit that you can lay out before YHWH to honor and magnify him and give thanks.

WORSHIP AND ADORE YHWH. As your own spirit quiets down before his presence, put yourself in Moses' sandals as he approaches that burning, unconsumed bush. You, too, are on holy ground. Just pause and wait in the holiness of his presence. Let his holiness seep over into your being and make you holy. Ask him to open the eyes of your heart.

WAIT IN ANTICIPATION. Wait so that his passionate love care and compassionate jealousy embrace and permeate you. Wait while YHWH leads you into the depths of his own person and permits you to walk with him as he calls into being the things that do not yet exist.

SEE BEYOND. He lives without the time distinctions we call past, present or future. He takes our hand and we together engage that great dance of life that enfolds every falling leaf and sick child, every earthquake and roaring tsunami, every genetic discovery and uncertainty principle, every first blush of love and passing of aged saints. Everything is in him whom we call YHWH, everything is through him, by him and for him, and everything adheres to him in whom we live and move and have our being.

Chapter Seven

THE LORD

From Exodus 19 to 34 we find the greatest self-revelation of YHWH's person and character apart from his self-revelation in Jesus. It started three months after leaving Egypt with YHWH instructing Moses and all the people in how to approach him so they would not needlessly die. Before ascending the mountain, Moses built an altar and set up twelve stone pillars representing the twelve tribes of Israel. There they offered both burnt offerings and fellowship offerings. The animals' blood was to provide atonement for sin and the grain offerings were to enjoy the fellowship and presence of YHWH together. Following the covenantal pattern, Moses took the blood and sprinkled it upon the Book of the Covenant, reading the contents to the people. This included the Ten Commandments in chapter 20. They all made a commitment to YHWH and his Covenant: "We will do everything YHWH has said; we will obey." (Exodus 19:8 and 24:7).

ENCOUNTERING YHWH THE LORD

With the Mosaic Covenant now in effect, Moses, Aaron, Nadab, Abihu and the 70 elders of Israel ascended the mountain and there together gazed upon the ELOHIM of Israel, with pavement like sapphire under YHWH's feet, clear as the sky itself (Exodus 24:9-10). YHWH then told Moses to ascend further. As Moses ascended further with Joshua his aide, a cloud descended and YHWH's glory settled down on Mt. Sinai for 6 days. On the seventh day, YHWH called to Moses to enter the cloud and ascend to the top of Sinai. The Israelites watched YHWH's glory, like a consuming fire, on top of Mt. Sinai. Moses ascended further, transfixed by the cloud that descended and covered Sinai's peak.

Moses remained there for forty days and nights and received YHWH's instructions for living. There YHWH insisted that Moses receive the Sabbath as a sign between him and YHWH, for all generations, so all would realize that it is YHWH alone who makes Israel holy. Moses absorbed everything that YHWH said to him and all the covenantal words he heard: the terms and stipulations of the covenant celebrated between YHWH and Israel. Then YHWH gave Moses two stone tablets inscribed by Elohim's finger, the tablets that contained the Ten Commandments so Israel would follow YHWH with love and understanding.

THE WORSHIP REBELLION. While YHWH took 40 days to form his Tabernacle-vision in Moses, the people grew weary of waiting, guessing that YHWH could not protect Moses and that wild animals had eaten him or that Moses had abandoned them, leaving them as fugitives in a strange wilderness. They demanded of Aaron a more powerful god, like those of Egypt, a gold bull-calf to worship and lead them back to Egypt. Aaron gave in and then instructed the people to take off all gold earrings, the treasures received from the Egyptians during the Exodus—the gold and silver that later would be needed for building the Tabernacle (Exodus 32:1-6).

Aaron took their gold and fashioned an idol, a golden bull-calf, just like the ones they had worshiped in Egypt. The people came together to party early in the day, sacrificed burnt offerings and offered fellowship offerings. They cast off all instructions and restraints learned from YHWH during their six-week trek out of Egypt, sat down to eat and drink, and got up to indulge in sexual revelry—the very same worship style practiced among Egyptians on their holidays.

Notice that the object of idol making was to worship: to replace worship of YHWH with the bull-god of Egypt, symbol of sexual life and power. They had not made the switch into YHWH worship, the True and Living God. Once again, the Scriptures focus attention on worship as the key to comprehending YHWH, his purposes on earth and his love care for his people. The strength of YHWH's reaction to Israel's idolatry matched exactly his hatred of all satanic deceptions that seduce people today into preoccupation and worship of the natural order. Such earthy worship leads directly to YHWH's corrective judgment that Paul expounds in Romans, chapter one.

INTERCESSION, JUDGMENT, FORGIVENESS. Idolatry infuriates YHWH like no other sin, for it despises all the work and anguish YHWH experienced in bringing us to himself. It is like saying to YHWH, "We put no value whatsoever on you, your ways, your purposes, your sacrifices for us."

YHWH instructed Moses to descend the mountain, where he found the worship-rebellion in progress in the encampment. At this point, YHWH's anger burned with a fire-like ferocity. He would simply wipe off the earth this nation of rebellious slaves and rebuild his own vision of a worshiping nation with Moses as the leader (Exodus 32:7-10).

But Moses sought the favor and the grace that he knew lay within YHWH's person. Moses complimented YHWH for bringing Israel out of Egypt with signs and wonders and asked almost naively, "Why should you be angry with your people? Because if your fierce anger destroys this nation, then the Egyptians will accuse you of evil motives in leading Israel into the wilderness of Sinai. They will say that you rescued them from Egypt just to annihilate them here in the desert of Sinai" (Exodus 32:11-12). Moses further reminded YHWH of his promise to give this land to Israel, from the Nile to the Euphrates. Such intercession turned YHWH's anger away from Israel. He relented and cancelled the wipe-out scheduled for Israel. But he did give instructions to the Levites to kill 300 of those involved in the sexual, idolatrous worship-revelry.

The next day, Moses confronted Israel with the greatness of their sin and headed up the mountain to see if YHWH would indeed forgive the people (Exodus 32:30-34). Moses begged YHWH to forgive their sin. And if YHWH wouldn't relent, then Moses would offer himself as the first to be killed in YHWH's outpoured judgment. He actually asked to be blotted out of YHWH's book. But YHWH graciously responded that he himself would blot out of his book only those who sinned against him. YHWH accepted Moses' intercession for the people, an awesome precursor and picture of the Calvary drama many centuries later with Jesus of Nazareth.

God's glory is God's goodness

REQUEST FOR YHWH'S VISIBLE GLORY. After placing a plague on disobedient Israel, YHWH demanded they strip themselves of all ornaments (Exodus 33).

YHWH then met with Moses in a tent just outside the Courtyard encampment. As Moses entered that tent, YHWH's presence descended in a cloud and stood at the entrance. Then all Israel rose up, each at his own tent, to worship the YHWH of Israel. There, YHWH spoke face to face with Moses, as a man with his friend. Joshua, his young aide, remained there in the tent.

Moses asked YHWH, "If you are pleased with me, teach me your ways so that I may know you and continue to find favor with you." Notice all that Moses asked of God: (1) that YHWH teach him his own ways; (2) that he (Moses) might come to know him (YHWH); (3) that he might find favor before YHWH; (4) that YHWH's presence might accompany him and all of Israel.

Moses pressed in on YHWH. He had seen the heart of YHWH—both his furious anger and compassionate forgiveness—and he wanted to know more and said that he wouldn't go anywhere unless YHWH's presence went also. He recognized that YHWH's presence distinguished Israel from all people groups on earth. YHWH responded that his presence would accompany Moses to give him rest in his work. YHWH assured Moses, that he was pleased with him and knew him by name.

Moses then asked to see YHWH's glory, that is, his own person, his own inner self. Moses' worship-obedience had drawn him into a desperate hunger for YHWH. Again, pleased with Moses' intense search to know him intimately, YHWH responded that he would cause all his goodness to pass in front of Moses so that Moses could see who he was. In effect, YHWH equated his own glory with his own goodness. What a moment of revelation to Moses! God's glory is God's goodness!

YHWH told him he would have mercy on those to whom he chooses to have mercy and he would have compassion on those to whom he chooses to show his compassion. This adds a profound quality to the name, YHWH. Here he began to fully reveal himself. Not only is he the "One who exists," the "One who relates," but also he is the "One who has mercy and compassion on people." The self-revelatory activity of YHWH continues in the midst of rebellion, judgment, intercession and grace, and still does today.

Often one sees, in print and on painted canvas, YHWH as a judgmental, vengeful, father-figure. How far from the truth! In Exodus 34, we encounter the greatest display of YHWH's person in easy-to-comprehend language. Ezekiel and Isaiah saw his presence in vision, in figurative form. But Moses saw and heard the person, not in terms of flesh and bones, but the inner essence of YHWH. This personal revelation happened nowhere else in the rest of Scripture until Jesus of Nazareth came out of the wilderness declaring, "Repent, for the Kingdom of God has drawn near!" Moses saw the person of YHWH and heard him declare the essence of his nature. No wonder that the faithful covenantal Jew until today places Moses as second only to YHWH himself!

The Name YHWH the Lord

YHWH told Moses to come up on the mountain and present himself there. He also said that no one could come up close and see YHWH's own face. Therefore he would cover Moses with his own hand in a rock crevice while his glory, the essence that lies within impassibly brilliant light, passed by. Moses could see his back, but no one could see his face except the One who lives in the bosom of his Father, Jesus of Nazareth.

There on Mt. Sinai, Moses stood with the two stone tablets in his arms. There YHWH came down in a cloud and stayed next to Moses and told him he would cause all his goodness-glory to pass in front of him. Then he proclaimed his name, YHWH, YHWH, The Lord, the Lord, full of compassion, grace, patience, covenant love, faithfulness, forgiveness, and accountability.

YHWH THE LORD – IS COMPASSIONATE. His compassion has no rationale or boundaries.

YHWH THE LORD – IS GRACIOUS. His enabling power changes us and helps us fulfill his purposes.

YHWH THE LORD – IS SLOW TO ANGER. He is patient and longsuffering.

YHWH THE LORD – IS ABOUNDING IN COVENANT LOVE AND FAITHFULNESS. This love means his love includes unbounded loyalty, no matter what.

YHWH THE LORD – MAINTAINS COVENANT LOVE TO THOUSANDS. He is sovereignly faithful to his own people.

YHWH THE LORD – FORGIVES LAWLESSNESS, REBELLION AND SIN.

YHWH THE LORD – WORKS OUT ACCOUNTABILITY. He does not leave the guilty unpunished, but brings about justice by calling all people to account for their sins.

This seven-faceted name of his own choosing is the name YHWH called himself, the name by which he is to be remembered from generation to generation. His name, his Goodness, is like a prism, through which the unapproachable light of his person shines, and refracts into the many layered different aspects of his nature. These seven facets we can identify and relate to as humans. But the overwhelming brilliance of his unshaded light—that would only destroy us.

Jesus, all that the Cloud carried of the personhood of YHWH—he alone strode the earth in human form

This name, YHWH, stands above all others in the Old Testament revelation and kept believing Israel on his pathway until the fullest revelation in Jesus of Nazareth. In John 8:58, Jesus actually calls himself YHWH. To the horror of legalists and the joy of believers, the YHWH of Exodus 34, Jesus, stands before the disciples and Pharisees bathed in Father's glory-goodness.

Only Jesus, all that the Cloud carried, all the inner personhood of YHWH, strode on earth in human form. The compassion and grace that Moses heard on Mount Sinai now stood in front of the disciples and crowds of Galilee. Grace and compassion became a person; patience and covenant love showered on all listeners;

abundance and maintenance of covenant love freely covered all who received him; forgiveness and accountability wrapped around broken and fearful people.

WORSHIPING YHWH THE LORD IN HIS GOODNESS

Meditate on YHWH's inherent worth and acts of love demonstrated to Moses and to us:

- YHWH shares his seven-fold name with those who want to know him.
- YHWH answers the desperate heart cry of to know his person.
- YHWH'S presence causes even mountains to tremble with earthquakes.
- YHWH invites us to eat with him in fellowship.
- YHWH invited Moses, and now us, to go further up the mountain to watch and enter into *The Cloud of His Presence* to form in the heart his vision for worshiping him.
- YHWH responds to those who seek to know him in his person, not just his mighty works. He shares the secrets of his person with those who ascend his mountain, wait before him and walk into the cloud.
- YHWH delights in those who ask to see his glory, his inherent goodness.
- YHWH confronts people who reject worshiping him, who replace him with idols made from the course of nature; he alone fashions correction, judgment, or punishment to match the seriousness of the offense.

REFLECT ON THE WORD "GLORY." In order to bring the term "glory" more into the realm of our comprehension, try thinking of "glory" in its interplay with "holiness." Holiness in itself is invisible to mortal eyes and needs the covering of glory so we can perceive it as light. Start with the idea that holiness is YHWH's inner nature and glory is the outward expression of holiness. Glory then is holiness wrapped in light. We can also say that Glory is Holiness embodied, like a garment covering a person. Holiness by Glory becomes visible. Glory is the outer garment of Holiness. Holiness is the inner essence of Glory and God's Person.

THANK AND PRAISE YHWH. Let your own awareness of YHWH and his glory lead you to give thanks for the inestimable privilege of bowing in his presence to worship him. Specifically, praise YHWH for each of the seven facets of his glory-goodness and holiness. Let your praise rise to him who shares his glory with mere humans: praise him for his compassion, grace, patience, forbearance, abundance of covenant love and faithfulness, maintenance of covenant love to thousands, forgiveness of lawlessness, rebellion and sin, working out justice for all.

ADORE AND WORSHIP YHWH. Peter, James, and John saw the unshaded glory of Jesus-Messiah on that mount of transfiguration. It came upon them with no effort on their part. Invite his glory to settle in on you in the same way!

> **Glory: holiness wrapped in light**

On the other hand, patiently waiting is another way of YHWH, the living God. Patiently ascend into YHWH's presence through the covenantal blood of Jesus the Lamb of God. Ask the Spirit to cleanse your conscience from all memory of sin. Worship unhurried, like Moses, until he bids you come into his presence and talk together.

THE LORD

WORSHIP AND ADORE. Now just wait in his presence and let all that he is flow into your whole being, all that you are. Let him fill that part of you made only for him. So be it! Amen!

Let his compassion embrace you.

Let his grace amaze and sustain you.

Let his patience encourage you.

Let his love and faithfulness fortify you.

Let his constancy and trustworthiness establish you.

Let his forgiveness humble you.

Let his justice give you hope for the past, present and the future.

Section Four

Worshiping YHWH in the Prophetic Era

This era has a forward-looking perspective that saw a greater work than had ever yet been accomplished by the hand of the Lord: a work of God performed in the heart that would move people to follow YHWH out of a heart love and commitment.

Encountering the Name of YHWH in Israel's History

The importance of a name in Israel cannot be overstated. YHWH stepped into history by covenanting with all creation as Elohim, then as YHWH Elohim as he chose to engage relationship with us personally.

To understand the significance of the Lord's name to Israel, look at the spontaneous exuberance of a worshiper in Psalm 9:10, who exclaimed: "Those who know your name will trust in you, for you, Lord, have never forsaken those who seek you." To know YHWH's name is to come to trust him as God. This epitomizes the cultural attitude towards names: to know a person's name is to know the person.

Other illustrations of encountering YHWH's name in Israel's history also reveal the significance of his name. In your family, your parents may have named their children to preserve family traditions, to honor certain relatives, living or deceased, or to express their own hopes for a particular child. But in Mid-Eastern cultures like Israel, people felt that a name revealed the essential identity of that person. Given that cultural perspective, one can understand why so much of revelation history revolves around the names of God. God wanted to reveal his inner person to all people and began to name himself, progressively, first to selected individuals and families, then to a small nation, and ultimately to the entire earth's population through his One and Only Son. His name is always linked to his character.

> **To know YHWH's name is to trust him as God**

In Israel's trek from Egypt to the Jordan's crossing point, Moses exhorted them to seek for the place where the Lord their God would choose to put his name (Deuteronomy 12:11). Where YHWH places his name is where you will find his person.

When King David ventured to return the Ark from the Philistines to the people of Israel, the writer of 2 Samuel 6:2 described the transfer of the Ark in terms of the name of God: "He and all his men set out from Baalah to bring up from there the Ark of God which is called by the Name, the name of the LORD Almighty, who is enthroned between the cherubim that are on the ark."

When Solomon wanted to build a Temple, he sent a message to Hiram, King of Tyre that he wanted to build a Temple for the name of the LORD his God. In Isaiah 42:8, the prophet quoted the LORD YHWH, "I am the LORD. That is my name! I will not give my glory to another or my praise to idols."

Both David and the Prophets, and especially Isaiah, Ezekiel and Jeremiah, had a similar perspective concerning the Mosaic Covenant that provided the fabric for constituting and maintaining the nation of Israel on its odyssey from slavery in Egypt to a sacral nation, dedicated to YHWH, his forever Name.

In addition, two other names were revealed during this time period: God our rock and the Ancient of Days.

ROCK: THE NAME THAT SPANS ALL OF ISRAEL'S HISTORY. Another Name that engages our heart is God our Rock. Throughout the history of Israel, from Genesis to Habakkuk, we find the people of God appealing to the one whose name is the ROCK, from the Hebrew word *hatsur*.

This name of Rock is linked to the self-revealed names of Elohim, YHWH, and El Shaddai. We find its first use in Genesis at the time that Jacob blessed his many sons.

> **God's name is Rock, our savior**

As he blessed Joseph in Hebrew poetry (Genesis 49:24-26), Jacob extolled the "Mighty One of Jacob, the Shepherd, the Rock of Israel...your father's God (Elohim), the Almighty (El Shaddai)." This recounting of YHWH's names called down on Joseph the greatest blessing among Jacob's sons, that of "the prince among his brothers."

In the Song of Moses, he extolled YHWH for his work over and among all nations on earth: "I will proclaim the name of the Lord YHWH. Oh praise the greatness of our God (Elohim)! He is the Rock, his works are perfect and all his ways are just" (Deuteronomy 32:3-4).

The Rock is Israel's Savior (Deuteronomy 32:15), the one "who fathered you" (32:18). There is "...no one holy like the Lord YHWH...there is no Rock like our God (Elohim)" (1 Samuel 2:2). David's song of praise in 2 Samuel 22:32 exclaims, "And who is God (Elohim) besides the Lord (YHWH)? And who is the Rock (*hatsur*) except our God (Elohim)?

The various Psalmists appealed to the Rock as the unchangeable, immovable, ever-merciful YHWH God of Israel, the One on whom they could always depend to fulfill his covenant with faithfulness (Psalms 18:2, 31; 19:14; 78:35; 89:26).

The Ancient of Days is YHWH-Elohim invading our space-time world

During Israel's prophetic period, Isaiah called on the Rock, Israel's eternal fortress (Isaiah 17:10; 26:4; 30:29; 44:8). Habakkuk appealed to the Rock of Israel, the One who would use the Gentile nations to bring judgment on Israel (Habakkuk 1:12). This Rock is our God!

ANCIENT OF DAYS: DANIEL ENCOUNTERS THE LIVING GOD. The Hebrew word for prophecy is to see a vision. It's a special word, not the common one, for "see." It means to experience a vision in which everyone understood the encounter as with the Holy One. Daniel 7:9-10, similar to the throne room scene of Revelation 4-5, records the encounter in which Daniel sees this vision and approaches the Presence of YHWH on his throne,

> As I looked, thrones were set in place and the Ancient of Days took his seat. His clothing was as white as snow; the hair of his head was white like wool. His throne was flaming with fire and its wheels were all ablaze. A river of fire was flowing, coming out from before him. Thou-

sands upon thousands attended him; ten thousand times ten thousand stood before him.

Another covenant, written on the heart

In Daniel 7:21-22, Daniel again speaks of the Ancient of Days, this time referring to lineage, a transfer of days. They decided on the phrase in English, Ancient of Days, to cover the verb, meaning "coming out of the ancient past" referring to YHWH Elohim invasion of our time-space world. The passage reads,

> As I watched, this horn was waging war against the saints and defeating them, until the Ancient of Days came and pronounced judgment in favor of **the saints of the Most High, and the time came when they possessed the kingdom.**

In Daniel YHWH is revealed as Prince of Princes, the Most Holy, the Living God, the Ancient of Days, the Great and Terrible God, the King of Heaven, the God of Heaven. He is an awesome God.

ENCOUNTERING ANOTHER COVENANT: THE COVENANT IN THE HEART

The prophets speak of another covenant, one written on the heart. In 2 Samuel 7:12-16, we read about an eternal aspect of David's kingdom, an aspect never anticipated in his original anointing as King over all Israel. Nathan the prophet spoke of a descendant who would build a house for YHWH's name, which was fulfilled by Solomon, David's son. However, the Word continued and revealed that YHWH would establish the throne of his kingdom forever, "Your house and your kingdom will endure forever before me; your throne will be established forever" (2 Samuel 7:16). This alone belongs to Jesus as King.

In Psalm 89, the writer Ethan spoke of another covenant. He spoke for his nation with jubilation and lament: joy for the reality of YHWH's covenant faithfulness and grief for some unnamed catastrophe that captured the nation. In the midst of verses 27-29, YHWH declared with expectation an encounter with the eternal covenant. He spoke about the coming Messiah-King, "I will appoint him my firstborn, the most exalted of the kings of the earth. I will maintain my love to him forever and my covenant with him will never fail. I will establish his line forever, his throne as long as the heavens endure."

In addition to the psalmist speaking of another covenant, Jeremiah also anticipated another covenant, one in which "I will put my law in their minds and write it on their hearts. I will be their God and they will be my people" (31:33). But it is Ezekiel who saw the Glory of Israel and wrote of YHWH's plans to demonstrate to the Gentile nations that he is the LORD, "... for the sake of my holy name, which you, Israel, have profaned among the nations where you have gone. I will show the holiness of my great name ....Then the nations will know that I Am the LORD, declares the Sovereign LORD, when I show myself holy through you before their eyes" (36:22-23).

In Isaiah he encounters the names of Immanuel, Wonderful Counselor, Mighty God, Everlasting Father, Prince of Peace, A Rod, a Stem, a Branch, a Diadem of Beauty, a Foundation. In Ezekiel 36:24, YHWH outlined many features of his plan to show himself holy among the nations: "I will gather you ... I will cleanse you...I will give you a new heart...I will put my Spirit in you ... I will move you to follow my decrees...I will save you from your uncleanness ... I will increase the fruit of the trees and the crops of the fields ... I will cleanse you from your sins."

These features sound exactly like the New Covenant of our Lord and Savior Jesus Christ. Though Moses' Torah may have held Israel rigidly to YHWH's standards, we see that something else is being planned. This New Covenant has features that resolve the incompleteness of the Mosaic Covenant.

In the coming chapters you will see how Isaiah and Ezekiel, as prophets, carried a special sense for recognizing God's saving activity and encountering his names and Presence accordingly.

Chapter Eight

QADOSH, THE ONE WHO IS HOLY

Of all the prophets, Isaiah saw most clearly the sovereignty of YHWH over generations of nations and peoples, and understood most deeply YHWH's holiness as it touched earth's peoples. Isaiah used the name, "The Holy One of Israel" 26 times, a title found in the rest of the Old Testament only 6 times. Isaiah clearly saw the holiness of YHWH. Isaiah characteristically used the name "The Holy One" to express the awesome person, YHWH, who intervened in human history. He intervenes particularly into the lives of ordinary people to bless and heal or call into his presence; in agriculture and military battles, to dispose all things according to his own purposes.

> **Isaiah used the name Qadosh more than four times as much as the rest of the Old Testament combined**

Isaiah, as eyewitness to current and future history in the Middle East, recognized that YHWH brought the essence of his own nature to bear on our earthly existence. YHWH's holiness broke the resistance of all things so that his purposes and his will transform willing followers into grateful children, wholly engaged in what pleases YHWH.

The concept that still staggers the mind and heart of this writer is not that of God living in the splendid isolation of his own holiness. Many a religious philosopher has projected that argument.

The concept that astounds the mind and imagination is that the One who is Holy, who lives in the impeccable purity of holiness, would step out of his native environment and cross over to this solar system, and related galaxies, in which the primary species of mankind has decided to live in anything but the holiness that characterizes the One who is Holy.

The unanswerable question remains: Why would the One who is perfect in his holiness cross that great divide into our environment characterized mainly by pollution of heart, mind, soul, body and environment? Yet, the Scripture assumes and arms this astounding truth. God left his own home of holiness and actually took on a human nature and body to live and work in our pollution-ambient.

Encountering YHWH with Isaiah

Isaiah's ministry took place during the emerging threat of the westward expansion of the Assyrian Empire. In about 722 BC, with pain and compassion, Isaiah watched Assyria attack and destroy Damascus, Israel's center for the northern ten tribes. All inhabitants were enslaved or killed, and the capital city destroyed forever as the center for the ten northern tribes. Further, Isaiah foretold the yet-to-come destruction of Jerusalem in 586 BC, capital of the two southern tribes. He also told of the restoration of Israel after 70 years of captivity in Babylon. He continued his ministry until 680 BC.

Isaiah's call was to a people whose hearts had turned away from the Lord. He consistently prophesied words of repentance and hope and the people consistently turned away. What a grief to YHWH's and Isaiah's hearts. It was in this context that Isaiah experienced a vision of YHWH's holiness in the year that his king Uzziah died in 740 BC.

EXPRESSIONS OF HIS PRESENCE: THE THRONE ROOM SCENE. In Isaiah 6, no doubt Isaiah looked into the heavenly realm and saw the throne room scene that Ezekiel, Daniel and John also testified to in their visions. To read this vision draws the presence of God to the worshiper, and, thus, forever validated Isaiah as a legitimate prophet for all Israel. The Temple in which Israel worshiped, first in the desert Tabernacle, then in Solomon's Temple and finally in Herod's Jerusalem Temple, that structure represented a physical expression of the Heavenly Temple that surrounds YHWH's presence in heaven. Isaiah saw that same Heavenly Temple as Moses did on Mt. Sinai along with the on-going worship scenario.

Isaiah saw YHWH, seated on a throne, high and exalted, and the train of his robe filled the temple. Isaiah perceived YHWH as absolute sovereign and surrounded by seraphim, creatures of incandescent burning purity, creatures that have six wings that they use to cover their faces and feet, and to fly. These are similar godly creatures to those in Ezekiel's visions in chapters 1 and 10, and the living creatures of Revelation 4 and 5. Isaiah's chapter 6 vision revolutionized his perspective about YHWH, from a sovereign Deity over a chosen nation, to a sovereign Deity over a ruined, deserted Jerusalem—whose holy seed would be the stump leftover in the land.

> **Human creation shudders in a vain attempt to contain the intensity of YHWH's holiness**

The train of YHWH's robe filled the temple. To use an earthly metaphor, the robe that a king or emperor wears carries a visible and royal display of all virtues that ruler has by inheritance or accomplishment. So the train of the robe is that ruler's reputation and identity open for all to see. YHWH represents his entire nature and character, as well as all his creative accomplishments on the train of his robe that Isaiah described as filling the Heavenly Temple.

Isaiah then portrayed the effect of the seraphim's worship of YHWH's presence in the Heavenly Temple. The seraphim expressed YHWH's inherent nature of purity and sovereignty by calling to each other: "Holy, holy, holy is the LORD Almighty. The whole earth is full of his glory." The triple use of "holy" makes emphatic the infinite dimensions of YHWH's purity, or holiness, that almost ineffable quality of being so non-human, so far outside of our space-time continuum that we simply cannot identify with him. Yet he comes to Isaiah in clearly identifiable shape, motion, and words, and forever reveals himself as the God who compassionately covers peoples' sin and graciously commissions them to serve his purposes on earth. Isaiah's use of the name Shaddai, Sovereign One, describes YHWH's total power and lordship over the universe he created.

As they cried out "Holy, holy, holy," the doorposts and thresholds of the Temple shook and trembled at YHWH's presence. YHWH's holiness affects all his creation. The intensity of his holiness is such that the human creation shudders in a vain attempt to contain his uncreated and immeasurable holiness. Furthermore, the entire Heavenly Temple filled with smoke. We know that when Moses saw YHWH's presence on Mt. Sinai, he described it as the entire mountain trembling with fire and smoke. Isaiah entered into that same experience: YHWH's presence caused all creation to quake, to quiver at the intensity of his person. In his vision, Isaiah saw the smoke of his presence as the stunning realization gripped him that he was unclean before YHWH's holiness. He saw this as the Cloud of His Presence, the very presence of YHWH himself.

ISAIAH HEARS AND RESPONDS TO YHWH'S PRESENCE. The shattering experience of seeing YHWH's presence overwhelmed Isaiah. The burning purity of holiness, the exaltedness of the person he gazed on, and the glory of the brilliant seraphim proclaiming the holiness of YHWH's person—all this combined to bring Isaiah into an appropriate humility before the Living God. He remembered the belief that anybody who saw God would die immediately. So he cried out:

- Woe to me!
- I am ruined!
- I am a person of unclean lips, heart and life.
- I live among a people of unclean lips, hearts and lives.
- My eyes have seen the King, the Almighty.

Immediately upon Isaiah's recognizing his own impurity, one of the seraphim flew to Isaiah with a live coal in his hand, taken from the altar in YHWH's presence. The seraph touched Isaiah's mouth with a live coal and declared him clean, demonstrating that YHWH had taken away his guilt and atoned for his sin. This age-old principle works out before us: in the person of YHWH's son Jesus when a person believes what YHWH says. Then YHWH declares him guiltless and his sin is erased. Abraham also experienced this when he "believed the Lord, and he credited it to him as righteousness" (Genesis 15:6).

The vision, the sense of uncleanness in contrast to YHWH's purity, the humbling of one's self, the cleansing from YHWH's presence—all of this brought Isaiah to a position in which he could receive YHWH's purposes and plans for his life on earth. So YHWH's voice declared clearly in Isaiah 6:8: "Whom shall I send? Who will go for us?" YHWH was looking for a servant to fulfill the destiny of carrying out YHWH's purposes on earth. And Isaiah responded immediately, "I'm here! I'm ready! Send me!"

YHWH's Purpose for Isaiah. YHWH then disclosed his purposes for Isaiah: He was to go and tell YHWH's people that they are "always hearing but never understanding, always seeing but never perceiving." In Isaiah 6:10, he is then told to make the people's hearts calloused, make their ears dull, and close their eyes. If Isaiah did not carry out this mandate of YHWH, the people might otherwise "See with their eyes, hear with their ears, understand with their hearts, and turn to YHWH and be healed (Isaiah 6:10)."

Isaiah's prophetic words, effectual and living as they were, would have a judgmental effect on the unbelieving hearers. This Word-judgment made their hearts calloused, their ears dull and their eyes ineffective and prepared them for Assyria's intervention and eventual destruction of Jerusalem. The Pharaoh of Egypt experienced the same hardening effect of Moses' words, when he rejected YHWH's command to let his people go that they might worship him. To reject YHWH's word is to invite a judicial blindness upon one's heart and mind that parallels Paul's comments in Romans 1:18-32.

With his heart aching over the loss of his monarch-ruler King Ussiah, and dread at the implication for his beloved nation, Isaiah asked YHWH, "How long will I do this?" (Isaiah 6:11). YHWH answered that Isaiah was to continue his prophetic teaching until even the land itself lay destroyed. And in the midst of that horrendous destruction, YHWH himself would preserve a stump, his holy seed, like a felled tree in a forest leaves its stump. In the succeeding 60 chapters, Isaiah spelled out in detail YHWH's intervention, through Assyria and Babylon, in Israel, in Judah and in the surrounding nations, in the midst of innumerable scenarios of judgment.

GOD'S NAMES TO ISAIAH

Isaiah clearly brought to light YHWH's Word about his Name as Qadosh, Holy. This name most profoundly affected Isaiah's whole life and ministry.

YHWH – THE HOLY ONE OF GOD. The term "holy" means that which inspires awe, even dread, and one that should be treated with caution. The holy nature of YHWH is *qadosh*. The verb *qadosh* signifies the encroaching Presence of God. Anything that YHWH inhabits or uses automatically becomes holy because he is holy. For instance, ground becomes holy because YHWH is there (Exodus 3:5); the weekly Sabbath is holy; the nation of Israel is holy; the altar is holy within the Holy Place and the Holy of Holies.

As no one can make himself holy, YHWH declared: "I AM YHWH who makes you holy" (Exodus 31:13). He sanctifies us, cleanses us, and he sets us apart as holy. As we walk in gentle obedience to his ways, he makes us into his own holy image. This dictum guided Israel's thinking: You shall be holy because I AM HOLY (Leviticus 11:45).

No one can make himself holy. God alone does it

In Classical Hebrew, the word *qadosh* signifies "to be pure, clean, holy or sacred." The meaning starts from an idea of separation or withdrawal. People or things that are withdrawn or separated are *qadosh*. And YHWH lives in a dimension so apart from our space-time world, that he is *qadosh* by nature. The LORD-YHWH built into earthly Israel a complex system of clean and unclean food, utensils, and activities. To be clean in lifestyle opened God's people to YHWH's grace-work to make them holy. Today he teaches us how to separate ourselves from the unclean of the world system as an expression of his holiness that he is imparting to us. Holiness refers to character, the inner essence of the person; clean-unclean refers to lifestyle or activities of life. Only Jesus exemplifies and demonstrates this life style.

The One who is holy, the One revealed in the person of Jesus Christ, lives in an environment where no other quality of life takes precedent except holiness. In the Lord's presence, the quality of life that we call holy or holiness pervades unchallenged and tolerates nothing less than the perfection of God's purity. Therefore nothing or nobody continues in the Holy One's presence besides that which matches the Holy One's original holiness. Picture his holiness as purity or cleanness that purifies or vaporizes anything that lacks even one iota of being holy.

There are two occasions in the New Testament when Jesus was called by this holy name. First, the unclean spirits in the demonized man in the synagogue called out: "What do you want with us, Jesus of Nazareth? Have you come to destroy us? I know who you are—the Holy One of God" (Mark 1:24 and Luke 4:34). Apparently, the demonic forces knew Jesus by this name.

> **Isaiah saw Messiah as the One who met the desires of Father's purposes and delights his heart**

Also, in John 6:69, Simon Peter responds to Jesus' question about their leaving him with: "LORD, to whom shall we go? You have the words of eternal life. We believe and know that you are the Holy One of God." Here, out of personal revelation and relationship, Peter encounters and acknowledges the Name for Jesus as the "Holy One of God." A measure of the character of holiness inherent in Jesus of Nazareth finally broke through to Peter's understanding and brought him to his knees in humble worship and confession of faith.

ISAIAH ENCOUNTERS MORE OF YHWH'S CHARACTER IN OTHER NAMES. It was out of the context of YHWH's holiness that YHWH consequently revealed to Isaiah many other aspects and Names of his character. The four "Isaiah Hymns," found in 42:1-7, 49:1-7, 50: 4-11, and 52:13-53:12, prophetically craft for the reader a mosaic of extraordinary names and virtues that characterize the Messiah. Look at these hymns carefully, words that so guided Isaiah and formed his prophetic eyesight into YHWH's nature.

Here you will find him as Servant, Ruler, Messiah and so much more. He comes to create a new man in every believer, and a new nation, the church. This was never before comprehended or expressed, except in figure by Old Testament kings, prophets and apostles.

Isaiah saw Messiah as the One who has met the desires of Father's purposes and delighted his heart, the Holy One from YHWH. Isaiah 53 is a well-known description of YHWH's heart poured into his one and only Son, Jesus, the Messiah for all ages and peoples.

He saw him coming to earth as Israel's Savior and Deliverer, and as Redeemer and Sovereign Lord for all Gentile and non-covenant peoples on earth. He is the one who offered his back to those who beat him. His life, heart, and actions as Redeemer and Deliver won the heart of Father. (Isaiah 49:7)

In several of these hymns Isaiah portrays YHWH as the Servant in whom YHWH displays his splendor. Isaiah 42:1 says, "Here is my servant, whom I uphold, my chosen one in whom I delight; I will put my Spirit on him and he will bring justice to the nations." He is our example in his life laid down, who only did the will of the Father.

Isaiah portrayed him as the Ruler and Tender Root out of Dry Ground. He was without beauty or majesty, whose very life YHWH made a guilt offering. He is also the Branch of the Lord (Isaiah 4:2). He was and is the only Messiah, hope for all peoples. He is the Ruler today and all the days to come.

Worshiping YHWH-Qadosh with Isaiah

Prepare. First, place yourself alongside Isaiah in chapter 6 as YHWH's blazing, triumphant presence broke in on Isaiah's body, soul, mind and spirit.

Thank and Praise YHWH. Present to YHWH your personal process that parallels Isaiah's encounter. Place yourself in Isaiah's shoes and respond to YHWH as Isaiah responded. Let the awareness of his holiness bring out your own awareness of sin and inadequacy. Declare to the King of Heaven your own need and listen for his words of gracious forgiveness and cleansing. Jesus has atoned for your sin—completely, totally, once and for all. Let the fertile ground of this encounter supply you with seed that extols the broad and deep compassion that surges from YHWH's holiness. Declare to him the worthiness that is uniquely his! Let your response to YHWH's presence parallel that of Isaiah: "Here I am, LORD, send me to accomplish your purposes!"

Worship and Adore YHWH. Wait in quietness before the LORD. Just wait in his presence. Let the loving fire of his holiness touch your awareness. Open to him who alone is holy. Let his holiness make you holy:

- The presence of the One who alone is holy.
- The presence of the One who raises up leaders and deposes them.
- The presence of the One who sees the death of his saints as precious.
- The presence of the One who commissions us to serve him all our days even for difficult purposes.
- The presence of the One who surrounds himself with seraphim to accomplish his purposes.
- The presence of the One whose high and holy throne draws us up into his exaltedness and holiness, to forever bow before his Throne.

Chapter Nine

QABOD, THE GLORY OF ISRAEL

Three different deportations stripped Jerusalem and the surrounding area of educated, wealthy and productive people. The first deportation in 605 B.C. was when Nebuchadnezzar, King of Babylon, laid siege to Jerusalem and took home some articles from Solomon's Temple along with selected youth, including Daniel (2 Chronicles 36:5-7). The second deportation in 597 B.C. occurred when Nebuchadnezzar laid siege to Jerusalem and captured about 10,000 Jews, including Ezekiel (2 Chronicles 36:9-10). With the third deportation in 586 B.C., the Babylonians completed their work of destroying Jerusalem and carried away all the articles of the temple and anything of value. Those who escaped the sword were made slaves (2 Chronicles 36:15-20).

> **Ezekiel saw the *qabod*, the glory of God, that should have only been in the Holy of Holies**

Modern scholarship dates Ezekiel's thirteen prophecies from July, 593 BC to April, 573 BC. Ezekiel's book of prophecies, chapters 1-24 deal with YHWH's impending judgment on Jerusalem. Chapters 25-32 deal with YHWH's judgments on various nations surrounding Israel. Chapters 33-48 deal with YHWH's vision for restoring Israel to a place she had never known under Moses' Law and Solomon's kingdom.

QABOD, THE GLORY OF ISRAEL

ENCOUNTERING QABOD, THE GLORY OF ISRAEL, WITH EZEKIEL

It is into this setting that Ezekiel, at 30 years old, began to see and record his prophetic word-visions from YHWH by the River Kebar, while living among the exiles of Jerusalem. The intensity of Ezekiel's vision validated him as a prophet before the covenant people. Ezekiel experienced YHWH's actual presence, heard him speaking—and yet survived. Most prophetic writers shared the words they heard or saw in vision form from YHWH, but not the presence that Ezekiel encountered. Ezekiel saw the *qabod*, the glory of God, the visible presence that should have only stayed within the Holy of Holies over the Ark of the Covenant. The intensity of YHWH's presence in the prophetic word spoke immediately to scribal leaders, a non-priestly people, and authorized the speaker as a genuine prophet. Thus YHWH launched Ezekiel into his prophetic work when the vision came upon him. He functioned as YHWH's prophet to Israel in Babylon for about 40 years and died there without actually seeing the fulfillment of his prophetic words concerning the restoration of Jerusalem.

Ezekiel's glimpse of YHWH ranks alongside the prophetic visions of Moses in Exodus 33-34 and Isaiah in Isaiah 6. They all saw YHWH's presence. They all struggled to describe what they had seen in inadequate, human language. Each time they encountered YHWH in his self-revelation, they recorded for us the form, color and motion, the indescribable and ineffable YHWH. When we link these prophets with John's vision of the Son of Man in Revelation 1 and the Throne Room scene of Revelation 4 and 5, we begin to experience with them the awe and the dread that any human feels in the presence of YHWH.

EZEKIEL'S FIRST VISION OF YHWH'S THRONE AND THE FOUR LIVING CREATURES. In the first part of Ezekiel's vision recorded in chapter one, he saw a theophany of YHWH Qabod in the form of a giant windstorm, like an enormous thunderstorm, coming out of the north, an immense cloud mass full of flashing lightning with dazzling light surrounding it. He saw in the center of the fiery cloud something that looked like glowing metal. And in the midst of the fiery metal he saw four forms that looked like living creatures, similar to those described in Revelation 4:6-8.

The form of these creatures looked like that of a human, but each of them had four faces and four wings. Now imagine a squared-off pole with four sides. Ezekiel saw a different face on each of the four sides of each pole. The living creatures all had straight legs, but their feet looked like calves' hooves. On each side, under their wings, they had human hands, and with their wings they touched one another. Consider the depth and breadth of Ezekiel's vision. Let the forms, colors, and motions fill your heart and mind with his glory.

- **FACES.** Each of the four living creatures had four distinct faces. One face looked like a human face that looked straight ahead. To the right of the human face Ezekiel saw a lion's face. To the left of the human face he saw an ox's face. On the backside Ezekiel saw the face of an eagle.
- **WINGS.** Each living creature had four wings. Its wings spread outward and upward. Two wings were used for touching the other Living creature on each side, and two wings for covering its own body. Under the expanse, the living creatures stretched their wings, both towards each other and to cover their bodies. When the Creatures traveled, the sound of their wings reverberated.
- **TRAVEL.** Each living creature traveled straight ahead wherever the Spirit would go, without turning as they went. At this point, our own constraints of space and distance fail to comprehend or match the description of how these Creatures traveled and we are left to the mystery of the divine Presence.

- **APPEARANCE.** Their appearance looked like burning coals of fire. Brilliant fire moved back and forth among the living creatures, like lightning, flashing as it went. The living creatures sped back and forth wherever they went, like flashes of lightning.
- **WHEELS.** Ezekiel saw a wheel on the ground beside each of the four-faced living creatures. All the wheels looked alike and they sparkled like chrysolite (a gem unknown to us). Each wheel consisted of a wheel intersecting a wheel, perhaps like a gyroscope. The wheels moved in any direction the four living creatures faced. For each wheel, Ezekiel described their rims as high and awesome, and full of eyes all around the rims.
- **MOVEMENT.** When the living creatures moved, the wheels traveled along beside them. When the living creatures rose, then the wheels rose with them wherever the Spirit would go, for the spirit. The identity and purpose of the living creatures remained within the wheels. When the living creatures moved, rose, or stopped, then the wheels moved, rose, or stopped with them.
- **THE EXPANSE THAT SEPARATES.** Above the heads of the living creatures Ezekiel saw an awesome expanse, sparkling like ice. Genesis 1:6 tells of an expanse that separated the waters above from waters below. In Ezekiel 1:22, the expanse separated the glory of YHWH above, that is, his personal presence, from the living creatures under the expanse.
- **THE VOICE.** Above the heads of the creatures and above the expanse, came a voice. Ezekiel heard YHWH's voice like the roar of rushing waters, like the voice of El Shaddai, The Almighty, like the tumult on an army in camp or on the move. At the voice, the living creatures all lowered their wings in awe and worship.
- **THE THRONE.** Then Ezekiel glimpsed a sapphire throne above the expanse and above the heads of the Living creatures. On that throne he saw a figure like that of a hu-

man. From the waist up that figure looked like glowing metal, as if it were full of fire. From the waist down the figure looked like fire, and brilliant light surrounded him. The radiance that emanated from him looked like a rainbow in the clouds on a rainy day.

> **Ezekiel's visionary experience was the appearance of the likeness of the glory of YHWH**

THE GLORY. Ezekiel called this entire visionary experience "the appearance ... of the likeness ... of the glory of YHWH." He fell face down to hear the voice of YHWH El Shaddai, the Lord Almighty. It was into this context that YHWH spoke and commissioned Ezekiel in chapter 2 to go to the Israelites, a rebellious nation, and speak YHWH's direct words.

EZEKIEL'S CONSEQUENT VISIONS OF THE THRONE. After Ezekiel experienced the first vision of YHWH's Glory Qabod by the River Kebar, and after his commissioning in chapter 2, YHWH gave to him a series of personal experiences with his own presence.

- THE FIGURE LIKE A MAN. Once again, as in chapter 1, Ezekiel sees a figure like a man with fire and glowing metal. Here the Spirit takes him in visions of God to Jerusalem where he beheld the glory of the God of Israel, YHWH Qabod.
- THE MAN CLOTHED IN LINEN. In Ezekiel 9:3-4 Ezekiel again sees the glory of the Lord. He also sees a man clothed in linen, a heavenly servant. He had a writing kit at his side, and received a commission from YHWH to mark the forehead of all Jerusalem's inhabitants who grieved over the idolatry and the loss of YHWH's ways among the people. All those without the mark on their

forehead would suffer the fate of Assyrian destruction. These are they who would go to Babylon as slaves. The man clothed in linen also appears in Daniel's account to supervise future judgments (Daniel 12:6).

- **THE THRONE AND THE COALS.** In Ezekiel 10 he again sees the throne above the expanse and told the man in linen to gather fiery coals from among the cherubim and scatter them over the city, a judgment by fire. Then the cloud of YHWH's presence filled the Temple and the court was filled with the radiance of YHWH's *qabod*. Ezekiel saw a wheel, sparkling like chrysolite, beside each cherub. All the wheels looked alike. Each wheel appeared to be a wheel intersecting a wheel, again like a gyroscope and the wheels traveled wherever the cherubim wished. Ezekiel heard that the cherubim called their wheels "the whirling wheels."
- **THE CHERUBIM.** The cherubim—their entire bodies, backs, hands, wings—were filled with eyes; in the same way all the wheels were filled with eyes, an indication that they see and know everything that happens. And the four faces of each cherub, similar to chapter 1, looked like a cherub, a man, a lion and an eagle. The only difference was that there was a cherub in chapter 10 and an ox in chapter 1. These cherubim and the wheels carried or bore YHWH's *qabod* to accomplish whatever YHWH purposed.

THE GLORY QABOD DEPARTS. The vision of chapter 1 overwhelmed Ezekiel as a personal display of YHWH's person or glory. But starting in chapter 8, Ezekiel watched in horror as Israel's elders went in under the Temple to practice their idolatry. He saw the coming slaughter of Jerusalem's inhabitants, those who did not carry YHWH's mark on their foreheads.

Then, before his eyes, YHWH's own presence, the Glory *qabod* of Israel, moved out and abandoned Israel to its own desires (Ezekiel

10:18). Because of the detestable practices of Jerusalem's elders, YHWH sent angel-warriors into the city to destroy all those who lacked YHWH's mark on their forehead. In Revelation 8:6, when the angels prepare to sound their trumpets of YHWH's purposes, an angel with a golden censer fills it with the prayers of believers. He then takes fire from the altar and hurls it down on earth's ecosystems to accomplish YHWH's purposes.

As the cherubim stood at the south side of the temple, YHWH Qabod arose above the cherubim who stood guard over the Atonement Covenant of the Ark and moved over the threshold of the temple. The Cloud filled the temple and the radiance of YHWH's Qabod filled the court (Ezekiel 10:4-5).

> **From this time on there was no glory in Israel; they were left to their own evil desires**

Then YHWH Qabod left the Temple completely, and paused over the cherubim. In worship, the cherubim spread their swings and arose. They paused, waiting the movements of the YHWH Qabod above them. Together they moved to the East Gate of the Temple. Then YHWH Qabod moved out of the East Gate and out of the temple completely and stopped above the mountain east of the city, probably the Mount of Olives (Ezekiel 11:23).

From this time on there was no glory in Israel; the covenant people were left without the physical presence of their God. Israel had now become just like the nations of the earth; God no longer lived among them. And Israel would not see YHWH's *qabod* glory again until Jesus of Nazareth left his wilderness test and came into Galilee (Matthew 4:12-17) declaring that he, the Servant of YHWH, brought Father's reign to earth! Ezekiel 11:19 also promised that, "I will give them an undivided heart and put a new spirit in them; I will remove from them their heart of stone and give them a heart of flesh." This was only fulfilled in Jesus the Christ.

God's Names to Ezekiel

The linguistic background for *qabod* means "be heavy" and by extension "be important." In Hebrew, people can be "caused to be heavy" or "honored" or "glorious," with the same word. The major Biblical usages focus on giving honor to YHWH. YHWH is the *qabod* of the righteous, that is, the glory of the righteous or godly believers.

YHWH – QABOD, POWER, AUTHORITY AND HONOR. The *qabod* of YHWH, the glory of the LORD, can also be a fixed phrase that stands for YHWH's power, authority and honor. It can also stand for the outward appearance of YHWH as he appears to his people as when he appeared to Moses, the Elders of Israel, and to the prophets after the giving of the Ten Commandments. The people said that "The LORD our God has shown us his glory and his majesty, and we have heard his voice from the fire" (Deuteronomy 5:24). At the giving of the Mosaic Law, YHWH's glory settled in on the mountain, looking like a consuming fire, and remained there for 40 days (Exodus 24:16).

YHWH – QABOD, GLORY JUDGMENT. Glory also releases judgment. When Korah, a Levite, with several Reubenites, became insolent and rebelled against Moses' authority, YHWH's glory judgment appeared to all Israel and destroyed the rebels by means of an earthquake (Numbers 16). Subsequently, all Israel arose in concerted opposition to Moses and 14,700 people died from the plague that YHWH's glory released.

YHWH – QABOD, BRILLIANCE, INTENSITY, AND RADIANCE. Glory can mean brilliance, or radiance in God's person. This was how John described Jesus in Revelation one. At the inauguration of Solomon's Temple, YHWH's glory filled the entire Temple with such intensity that the priests could not perform their services (I Kings 8:11). Ezekiel (43:5) spoke of YHWH's glory as inherent in the promises that will overtake Israel in the future. Isaiah (6:3) declares that YHWH's *qabod* fills the entire earth!

YHWH – QABOD, THE CLOUD OF HIS PRESENCE. Glory means YHWH's very presence, his person. Several contexts from Scripture illustrate this manifestation of his glorious Presence. The term glory as a synonym for YHWH's presence started in Exodus 16:10 at this grumbling rebellion against Moses' authority. The people looked towards the desert and saw YHWH's glory *qabod* appearing in the cloud. Instead of judgment, YHWH shared himself in the form of manna and instituted a 40-year supply of daily bread.

> **Wait until his presence is within or around you and then worship in silence**

At the inauguration of the Desert Tabernacle, the Cloud of YHWH's glory Presence covered the Ten of Meeting and came in and filled the Tabernacle. It was so powerful that everyone was driven out, including Moses (Exodus 40:34). Apparently the *qabod* glory hovered within the cloud and the cloud served to keep people from actually seeing the very person of God.

YHWH – QABOD, GOODNESS, MERCY AND COMPASSION. One very significant explanation for YHWH's glory is found in Exodus 33 when Moses asked God to show him his glory. Here the Lord responds with, "I will cause all my goodness to pass in front of you, and I will proclaim my name, the LORD YHWH, in your presence. I will have mercy on whom I will have mercy, and I will have compassion on whom I will have compassion." The *qabod* of YHWH is his goodness, mercy and compassion.

Qabod, the Glory of Israel

Worshiping YHWH in His Qabod Glory with Ezekiel

Thank and Praise YHWH. The entrance into YHWH's courts starts here. To give thanks and praise is to enter into his Temple, his House, the place where he lives. YHWH, when he hears our praise, opens the door for us to come into his presence. Pour out your heart in gratitude for all YHWH has already done in your life. By faith, shower him with thanks-praise for all you expect him to accomplish in and through you. Above all, lift you heart in gratefulness that he, YHWH, the God of the Universe, has shared his very nature with you. The Qabod YHWH has come to live in you!

Reflect on YHWH's *qabod* and pursue his living presence. You may come near to what the disciples experienced when Jesus of Nazareth metamorphosed before them into his incandescent glory and talked with Moses and Isaiah. In his presence, we lose all pretensions about our own worth, identity, and accomplishments. We fall down before him, as did Moses, Ezekiel, and John. Sometimes we remain like dead men until we hear his sweet and gentle voice that releases us from our self-preoccupation and draws us to gaze upon him through the face and words of Jesus, the Only-Begotten who lives in the bosom of Father.

Worship and Adore YHWH. Since holiness is YHWH's essence, and since glory is the outer garment of that holiness that people can see, express what you would like YHWH to show to you about his holiness-glory. Let your worship arise with your heart-adoration of who YHWH is. Wait until you sense his presence within or around you. Now worship in silence in his worthiness and holiness.

SECTION FIVE

WORSHIPING YHWH IN THE NEW TESTAMENT ERA

As you read details of the New Testament era, you may wonder about the change of emphasis on the names of God. Up to now, you have studied the major names by which YHWH was pleased to reveal himself to those who followed him in faith. But at this juncture in history, God's greatest and most complete name stood revealed in the person of Jesus of Nazareth. This was God's name from all eternity, now revealed in a human body, the God-man Jesus. All the qualities that belonged to the Living God also belonged to the Carpenter of Nazareth. Jesus is the Living YHWH incarnate. To speak and deal with Jesus is to speak and deal with the Living God.

Jesus related to his Father in a filial relationship, openly and consistently, and this name of Father helps us in our own thinking to largely complete the complexity inherent in the name of the Living God. This we find in Jesus' life and character, and in the apostolic writings—in abundance. All our New Testament documents look back to the grand occasion, the coming of Jesus, the sharing about his Father and the Kingdom he came to inaugurate. Yet it looked ahead to what the disciples never anticipated, the self-giving at the cross, followed by the resurrection and the Holy Spirit's descent at Pentecost. So now we will look at how Jesus identified the One who sent him to earth, the One who gave Jesus the Son his words to speak and his work to accomplish.

The Old Has Faded Away

The Old Mosaic Covenant was now obsolete (Hebrews 8:13). Its purpose and vitality have now been fulfilled and replaced by Jesus of Nazareth, Jesus the Christ reigning at Father's right hand. The Mosaic Law was only a shadow of the good things that were coming (Hebrews 10:1). Now the good things have arrived! The reality is here! Who needs a shadow when the sun has come out? The Law of God now stands written in our minds and on our hearts (Hebrews 8:10).

As Paul instructed in Galatians 3:22-24, the Mosaic Law served to show us our sin and "lead us to Christ that we might be justified by faith." The former regulation of the Mosaic Law had been set aside because it was now weak and useless; it never could have made anything perfect or complete (Hebrews 7:18). How difficult for us as New Testament believers to comprehend the experience of the Old Testament Mosaic Law, some 20 centuries after the writer of Hebrews penned these then-startling words.

John the Baptist marks the transition between the old and new. He never talked about the new covenant. His was a repentance not to receive the Spirit, but for forgiveness of sin. He didn't know about the Spirit because the Messenger hadn't arrived yet. Even in prison he asked if Jesus was the real one they were waiting for. Yet he was privileged to hear and see the very Presence of God.

The New Covenant Takes Over

Now the Spirit of God has baptized you and me into the Body of Christ and united us with him in the likeness of his death and in the likeness of his resurrection. The law of the Life-giving Spirit has now liberated us from the sin-death law (Romans 6:1-4; 8:1-2), thereby removing the final obstacle that kept him distant from his highest creation. We have been set free from the Mosaic Law, the way a widow stands released from her deceased husband, because we fulfill all the just requirements of the Law as we walk in the Spirit. We are free to be joined to and worship another, Jesus Christ. We serve God in the new way of the Spirit, not in the old way of the written code (Romans 7:6).

Best of all, as a result of all this behind-the-scenes work, Father has sought out those who would worship him in Spirit and Truth. He has called us to himself, forgiven our sins, separating us from our former lives of wearisome self-centeredness, and through the Spirit, ushered us into his very own presence. Through the Spirit, Father has built into us a bond of peace between him and us, a bonding that prompts us to call him Abba, "Daddy."

This filial bond now binds us to Father-Son-Spirit, and that bond has produced in us a yearning to know and worship the Living God. That bond makes our walk together not grievous, but an "easy yoke."

> **Our destiny is that joyful assembly of innumerable angels and believers in worship**

We become sensitive to Father's wishes and purposes. Though we often find ourselves at odds with Father, he moves us to crave his presence, to confess our sin and draw near again to him.

Relational Worship Is Our Destiny

How difficult it is for us, not only to comprehend the worship process of the Old Testament believers, but also to embrace the fullness of the relational worship to which YHWH, Father, has called us. We have not come to the Old Covenant, to the mountain that can be touched, but rather, we have come to the New Covenant, to Mount Zion, the Heavenly Jerusalem, the city of the Living God. We come to join with innumerable angels shouting in joyful assembly before YHWH Elohim El Shaddai. We come to encounter the Church of the Firstborn, to commune with men made perfect by the blood of Jesus. There we meet with YHWH, the Judge of all men, to see Jesus, the Mediator of a new covenant. And we walk free from sin because the sprinkled blood of Jesus speaks a better word of release than Moses ever knew (Hebrews 12: 22-24).

Our destiny is that joyful assembly of innumerable angels and believers in worship. It is noteworthy that we join a "joyful assembly." It is joyful because we all will have been remade in the spotless image of Christ himself. It is an assembly because we join all those who have come to experience the fellowship-worship that is the ambient of heaven. The longer we remain there, the deeper the intimacy and the more fervent the worship, the longer we have to appreciate the worthiness of him who died and rose again.

It is the worship that has changed from adherence to hunger, from following rules and regulations to unlimited and unhindered access to the Living God. The change of worship is based on the change of covenants, for worship is a heart attitude based on relating to Father, the God who is good. Let us follow in the steps of Jesus of Nazareth as he shows us how to relate with and worship the One whom Jesus named Father, the only One who is good (Matthew 19:17).

Father's Impartation to the Son as the Son of Man

The only One who is good became the Son of Man. The title "Son of Man," referring to the Messiah, appears rarely in the Old Testament. It is found only in Ezekiel and Daniel. In Daniel 7:13 he refers to Jesus the Messiah, "one like the son of man, coming with the clouds of heaven." Ezekiel's use of "son of man," was different as he used it as a "watchman" and not to refer to the Messiah.

> **Worship has changed from adherence to hunger, from rules to unhindered access**

It is not until Jesus was here and he was growing up in his mother's arms, cared for by his father, surrounded by his brothers and sisters that he went through the process of being human. Jesus developed an awareness of who he was as defined by Father who dwelt abundantly in him and was continually sharing his nature with him. In that sharing of his Nature with Jesus, Father gave him this title, Son of Man.

In the gospels, Jesus often talks about himself as Son of Man. In essence he was saying, "I am totally human just like each of you who are looking at me in this crowd today. I am the one who is characterized by the totality of being human. I am the son of humanity." Look at all the places in the gospels where Jesus applies the title of Son of Man to himself, and you will get a sense of the breadth of this title (see Matthew 16:27-28, Mark 14:62, Luke 22:69, John 3:13).

The corresponding phrase, "Son of God" is the son defined by his deity. The title, as Daniel thought of it and used it, was Messianic, that is deity. In Daniel 7:13 he explained it clearly, addressing Messiah as deity. It gave the rabbis and leaders in Israel all kinds of fits. It didn't work for their thinking. They thought

Messiah was some sort of a helper from God, and here Daniel saw him as the God man—the man who was God and the God who was man-- in two natures.

The foundation for understanding who Jesus is in the Scriptures is found in his two natures. He had the God nature and he had the man nature, Son of God and Son of Man. That's the consistent witness throughout the New Testament and carries over into our relationship with Jesus, Son of God and Son of Man. Philippians 2:5-8 tells us to have the same mindset as Jesus, Son of God made Son of Man, that in our personal relationships with one another we have the same attitudes and mindset as Christ Jesus who, being in very nature God, did not consider equality with God something to be grasped (used to his own advantage); but he made himself nothing by taking the very nature of a servant, being made in human likeness. And being found in appearance as a man, he humbled himself and became obedient to death—even death on a cross!" How awesome to be made like the One who first loved us. Enter his presence with praise and worship!

Chapter Ten

FATHER AND JESUS: FATHER AND SON

Jesus' primary activity on earth was to be one with the Father and do what he did and said. He named him Father. He was his Son. How Jesus and Father related to each other is the model for our love relationship with the Father-Son-Spirit. Then our worship springs from a deep sense of the filial relationship among Father and Son and Spirit.

> **Jesus talked about and demonstrated his filial relationship with Father**

Jesus talked about and demonstrated his own filial relationship with Father and never let it go. This topic pierced the heart like a sharp sword and laid bare the conscience of his listeners. Their minds must have wrestled with the idea that God and man could relate to each other as father-son. But Jesus had uncovered a yearning—an emptiness—a hunger that every listener could recognize. God had created them, both male and female, for that very purpose, that they might know God as Father and might together handle life on earth.

ENCOUNTERING YHWH FATHER THROUGH JESUS

As Jesus traveled through Galilee, he stopped at certain times on the trail, entering certain homes and addressing certain people. But nowhere did Jesus start each day with his agenda in hand, asking Father's approval on it. Rather, we see a constant attitude on Jesus' part to listen for the directive words that Father would share with him. Jesus had a lifetime attitude of waiting on Father, as the Psalmist stated: "Wait for the Lord; be strong and take heart and wait for the Lord" (Psalm 27:14).

Jesus had agreed to live out his life on earth by the power and direction of the Holy Spirit—the One who conveyed Father's heart and mind to Jesus. Pick any one of the hundreds of Jesus-events in the Gospels and watch Jesus unerringly step into a situation of Father's preparing. The Gospel writers arranged Jesus' actions and activities in strings of events that usually took place in the same geographical area. But the writers never tell us how Jesus chose to share certain teachings, go to certain places, heal certain people, and rebuke certain Pharisees. Rather, the answer is in Jesus' lifetime attitude: Wait on Father. This proved to be Jesus' source of strength and confidence—a steady patience and expectation that Father would direct him into those activities or teachings that would most disclose the person of Father and accomplish his purposes. Jesus waited on Father and responded to his direction so that Jesus was able to say to carping Pharisees, "I do only those things which please my Father."

> **Jesus had no pre-established daily agenda**

JESUS' ENCOUNTERED INTIMATE MOMENTS WITH FATHER

In the following Jesus-events, you can see the dimensions of relationship that Jesus walked in with his Father. Jesus had no pre-established daily agenda. They are all moments of intimacy, relational interludes, with worship as the ambient.

HIS BAPTISM. The Gospel writers all mentioned Jesus' baptism by John in the Jordan River (Matthew 3:13, Mark 1:9, Luke 3:21, and John 1:31). They realized, by the Spirit, the uniqueness of this encounter. All Israel, past and present, came together at this event: the Prophets represented by John the Baptist, the Law carried by the Pharisees, the Nation in the crowds, and Messiah in Jesus of Nazareth. John saw Jesus coming toward him and gave him another name, this time out of personal relationship and revelation, "Look, the Lamb of God, who takes away the sin of the world." As Jesus climbed the river bank, heaven itself opened and God's Spirit descended upon Messiah-Servant, just as Isaiah 11:1 and 61:1 recorded. The Servant of Isaiah 53 stood in the waters of baptism to identify with fallen humanity.

FATHER'S IMPARTATION TO THE SON. In chapters 5 and 6 of John's Gospel, Jesus explained in explicit detail his intimate relationship with Father and the Servant-commission that Father had given him to fulfill:

- The Son does only what Father shows him, what he sees Father doing.
- The Son speaks only the words he hears Father speaking.
- As Father raises the dead, so the Son gives life to whom he wishes.
- Father has given to the Son the authority to carry out all judgment.
- As Father carries life within himself, so also Father has given to the Son the authority to carry life in himself.
- Father grants him, the Son of Man, the authority to judge so that all people will honor the Son the same way they honor Father.
- If anyone does not honor the Son, then he is not honoring the Father, for Father testifies concerning Jesus.

The Spirit of Life who proceeds from Father's presence – the Spirit of Sonship – from the moment of conception, imbued Jesus with the immeasurable dynamic of Father's very self. Jesus' conception took place by the Spirit and the Spirit had filled Jesus all his days from the womb to the baptism. He had already clothed himself in a human body constrained by muscles with flesh, body and soul, and the spirit and heart, mind, will and emotions of human existence. But now Jesus received, without measure, the Spirit, the Breath of YHWH, as the mark of Father's confidence in him. This was the equipping for accomplishing Father's purposes.

IMPARTATION TO THE DISCIPLES OF RELATIONSHIP TO FATHER. The depth of Jesus' relationship with Father shines through in Luke 10:21. The context, at first glance, may seem incongruous. Jesus had sent his disciples to carry out his work, the work he had trained them to accomplish. But after the 72 returned from proclaiming the Good News of God's Kingdom, Jesus, full of joy through the Spirit, broke into personal adoration of Father, full of joy through the Holy Spirit. Jesus praised his Father for hiding the truth and the work of his kingdom from the wise, and for disclosing it to these "little children," his disciples.

Jesus was overjoyed to see Father's word and work accomplished by the disciples he had trained. But most especially, Jesus exulted over his private and intimate relationship with Father — that no one knew the Son except Father and no one knew who Father was except his Son. For Jesus knew that through the intimacy of the relationship he had started with his disciples, a relationship similar to the one he had with Father, his Father had imparted both his reign and his work. Jesus saw that the discipling process had taken root; it was producing what Father wanted.

> **Jesus demonstrated the flow between prayer and work**

JESUS' TIMES OF SEEKING FATHER ALONE.

Several examples show how Jesus demonstrated the flow between prayer and the call to work. First, in Luke 5:16 it reads, "But Jesus often withdrew to lonely places and prayed." Here Luke told how Jesus needed to have time alone without the crowds. He tied this come-apart prayer time in contrast to the crowds of people streaming to Jesus for healing.

It was "as he was praying" during his baptism that the Spirit descended on him and he heard Father's love words (Luke 3:21-22),. And just before Jesus appointed his twelve disciples to be apostles, he withdrew to a mountainside and spent the entire night with his Father. The next day, Jesus called his disciples together and chose twelve of them to be those who would eventually bear the leadership of the emerging Church (Luke 6:12-16).

Mark described another example of this prayer-pattern: "Very early in the morning, while it was still dark, Jesus got up, left the house and went off to a solitary place where he prayed" (Mark 1:35). Here you see Jesus' pattern of having a separate place where he shared intimate times alone with Father—apart from work and people.

After his disciples found him, Jesus was ready to take them on a teaching tour throughout Galilee, "preaching in the synagogues and driving out demons." In a similar way, Matthew 14:22-35 and Mark 6:45-61 tell how "After he had dismissed them (disciples), he went up on a mountainside by himself to pray …." Then, afterwards, Jesus walked on the water of the Sea of Galilee. The pattern is clear: times alone with Father prepared him to do what Father told him.

JESUS' EXAMPLES OF TALKING WITH FATHER

Jesus radicalized prayer for the hillside crowd who sat overlooking the Sea of Galilee in Matthew 5-7, the Sermon on the Mount. Jesus spoke to them as though YHWH were his Father! He wanted the people to pray in secret— to Father who is unseen. Jesus' listeners practiced prayer according to the precepts that Israel's priestly class commanded, that is, the prayer-phrasing used by the scribes, Pharisees and members of the Sanhedrin. But Jesus set a new example of prayer as talking with Father.

THE DISCIPLES' PRAYER. Luke 11:1 tells us that "One day Jesus was praying in a certain place. When he finished, one of his disciples said to him, 'Lord, teach us to pray ...'" Here Jesus showed his disciples the inner attitudes that underlie all prayer. For Jesus, prayer is an attitude of life: an anticipatory waiting on Father, a time to enjoy Father's presence, a time to be alone with Father, a time to be with his disciples in Father's presence, a spontaneous time of rejoicing over Father's goodness, a time for teaching Father's glorious, life-giving Words, a time of accomplishing Father's works on earth.

> **Prayer is the practice of relationship with YHWH who is Father**

In Matthew 6:5-15 and Luke 11:2-4, Jesus introduced prayer as not merely asking for one's needs. Instead, to Jesus, prayer is the practice of one's own relationship with YHWH who is Father. The listeners must have been shocked! From childhood, they were accustomed to prayers of repetitive phrases to show off an ability with words. Jesus simply turned their world upside down. He wanted them to receive God in their hearts, like Ezekiel prophesied, so they could live by God's perspective, not their own.

This relationship of Jesus and his Father became the point of contention between Jesus and the Pharisees, so that he was eventually killed for it. But here, Jesus pressed on and shared with the disciples his own prayer relationship to Father. In effect, Jesus told them: This is how I relate with Father every day and here's how you can touch your own filial relationship to Father in prayer!.

- **WORSHIP OF YHWH FATHER** Our Father who lives in heaven. Let your name be hallowed, sanctified, and made holy.
- **HUNGER FOR FATHER'S SOVEREIGN RULE.** Let your kingdom come, let your will and purposes be accomplished on earth, just like they are being accomplished in heaven.
- **RESOURCES.** Give us today our daily bread, our food and basic needs.
- **FORGIVENESS.** Forgive us our debts, our sins and offenses, as we also have forgiven our debtors, those who owe us apology or money or goods.
- **TESTING.** Lead us not into temptation [testing] but deliver us from the evil one.
- **EXPECTANT WORSHIP.** For yours is the kingdom, the power and the glory forever and ever.

> **Jesus' prayer life was not a time-out from serving Father**

The simplicity is amazing; the relationship striking and almost unbelievable. Jesus wanted the listeners to relate with Father the way he related with Father. From this moment on, believers in all generations have taken on this simple and relational set of requests and have delighted Father's heart ever since. By custom, we call this the "Lord's prayer." Actually, it is the "disciples' prayer," describing how Jesus said we should talk with Father.

PRAYING TOGETHER WITH HIS DISCIPLES. The Gospels record Jesus' habit of withdrawing from public scrutiny to spend time praying with his disciples. Jesus used such private times to impart to his disciples some of the most intimate secrets about himself and his kingdom, as the disciples' prayer just noted.

Put yourself into the context described in the gospels. We see that Jesus did not necessarily set out to have a "prayer meeting" with his disciples. Rather, as Jesus pursued his awareness of Father's activities for the day, the urge to engage Father in prayer took over as naturally as breathing. Jesus' prayer life was not a "time-out" from serving Father. On the contrary, Jesus' prayer life accompanied his activities in accomplishing Father's purposes and works.

Jesus' private times with his disciples did not consist in teaching popular or acceptable phrasing in prayer. Rather, their times of withdrawal from the public turned into times of seeing the "signs" that pointed to the Deity and Lordship of Jesus, that is, his own Sonship with Father. The disciples watched Jesus relate to and fellowship with his Father and learned that the common language between Father and Son is the language of prayer. This language the disciples wanted to learn; this language Jesus taught them.

Shortly after Jesus told the disciples that he would suffer many things, he invited each to take up his cross daily and follow him. Then Luke 9:28 relates that, "About eight days after Jesus said this, he took Peter, James and John with him …." and Jesus was transfigured before them. Jesus' human body at that moment experienced the transforming power of his eternal holiness and glory. Now the bonds of human life gave way to the eternal physics of God's unique presence.

GOD'S NAME OF FATHER, HIS REVEALED-BY-JESUS NAME

We find the best examples of the filial meaning of the name Father in Jesus' intimate prayer in John 17. Here we see the relationship between Jesus and his Father and hear the heart of Jesus for his Father, the disciples and future believers. We also clearly hear Father's heart for Jesus, integrated so completely into the fabric of Jesus' prayers. Here Jesus' closeness with Father results in an impassioned appeal in the Garden of Gethsemane for those he is about to leave on earth while he returns to Heaven.

FATHER. In John 17:3, Jesus shares the secret that eternal life is knowing Father. It's not doing things right or following all the laws left by Moses. Rather, it is to know Father, the only true God and Jesus Christ, whom he sent. In this way Jesus can then ask Father to glorify him "in the presence with the glory I had with you before the world began." Incredible revelations of truth are embedded in these words.

Jesus asks that Father glorify him by restoring to him the glory that he had always enjoyed in Father's presence, from before the beginning of the world (17:5). We can only touch the surface of what this means. In Jesus' pre-incarnate state, in the closeness of life as the Three-who-are-one and the One-who-is-three, we can only imagine the depth of intimacy that held the Three as One, an intimacy that Jesus graciously bequeathed to all his followers so that we may be one as he is one with Father (17:11).

Is this intimacy birthed in worship? Or, does worship emerge from the intimacy? Once a person has been born from above and received the Holy Spirit both are always present and available. We may not acknowledge the need for either or we may not practice either with Father. But Father has gone searching for those who will worship him in Spirit and Truth; that's how much he values intimacy birthed in worship and the worship generated from intimacy.

Following his intimate prayer for himself, Jesus began a series of requests for his disciples, and his future disciples. In John 17: 9-24, Jesus asked Father to give to his disciples everything that he, Father, had given to his Son:

- To protect them by the power of his name (17:11).
- To become one just like Father-Son are One (17:11, 21,23).
- To keep or guard them from the evil one (17:15).
- To sanctify, make them holy, by the truth (17:17).

- To be with Jesus so that they will see his glory (17:24).

With these requests answered by Father, the closeness of life with Father and the intimacy that Jesus enjoys with Father can now become the intimacy of all those who walk with him as his disciples. The goal of worship is intimacy with Father, just like Jesus showed us. And the goal of intimacy with Father is worship of the Living God, Father-Son-Spirit.

> **Faith is not a once-done act but a continuous gaze of the heart at the Triune God**
>
> A. W. Tozer,
> The Pursuit of God

MY SON IN WHOM I AM WELL PLEASED. John the Baptist was uniquely privileged to encounter God's Presence and hear his words, "This is my Son in Whom I AM well pleased." He heard the Name "Son in Whom I AM well pleased!" This reveals the filial relationship of Father and Son.

JESUS, THE I AM. In John 8:58, Jesus culminated these details of his intimate relationship with Father with this breathtaking revelation, that "Before Abraham lived, I AM," thus taking upon himself the name of the Great I AM in Exodus 3, the One who spoke from the burning bush. In John 10: 30, Jesus expresses the reality of his intimacy with Father by this simple statement: "I and the Father are one." Jesus has given to all on earth who follow him the blueprint of life in the Spirit, so that when one lives in this worshipful relationship with Father, then these are Father's impartations to his chosen ones. In John 10:30 and 36 he simply states "I AM God's Son....the Father is in me and I in the Father."

FATHER AND JESUS: FATHER AND SON

WORSHIPING YHWH FATHER IN JESUS' STYLE

REFLECT. Talk to Father about what you have gleaned from Jesus' relationship to YHWH Father. Meditate and talk to Father about each point.

GIVE THANKS AND PRAISE. Ask the Spirit to give you an unplanned, spontaneous moment of rejoicing before Father. Then pour out your thanks for what he has done and who he is. Multiply your thanksgiving for the process through which Father is building this faith-gaze into your life. The more you thank and praise and worship Father, the closer you draw to him and the more fervent his response to you.

WAIT QUIETLY FOR FATHER. Enjoy his presence. Permit him to enjoy your presence. Father has had this moment in mind since the time Adam and Eve chose to leave his presence. He relishes the time you spend with him. For this purpose he created you in his very image, to be one with him.

ADORE AND WORSHIP. You stand at the culmination of revelation-history. The fullness of the ages has come upon you. Father's Holy Spirit brings you graciously, gently to Jesus the Son, whose effective work on the cross now opens the way to Father. And you, hand-in-hand with Jesus, walk together into Father's presence so that together you may worship-adore Father, for Jesus is the Way to Father, and you have already come to know Jesus. The pinnacle of adoration-worship lies before you.

Chapter Eleven

GOD AND FATHER OF OUR LORD JESUS CHRIST

Worship during the Apostolic Age, from about 33 to 66 A.D., was lived out by the leaders whom Jesus had designated as apostles. These men carried Jesus' message and authority. They modeled for believers' the daily "life in the Spirit." The people of God accepted these apostles as God's leaders and examples. Therefore the apostles' experience of worship became the norm for the emerging Church, recognizing YHWH as the God and Father of our Lord Jesus Christ.

Like Jesus, the apostles learned synagogue worship from childhood. For them it took no great leap of faith to accompany Jesus into the Temple in Jerusalem and join worshipers led by priests. After Pentecost, Jewish Christians began to increase in great number and fill Herod's Temple daily, and not just for specified ceremonial days. One can only imagine the growing consternation of temple leaders to watch and hear these Jewish Christians as they worshiped by the new-found Spirit that rested upon them. For now the One who fulfilled the entire Old Testament also filled their hearts with new songs. All the Psalms became like a new songbook of the Spirit, played upon the hearts and tongues of these new Jewish Christians.

ENCOUNTERING YHWH IN APOSTOLIC ADORATION-WORSHIP

The move from Old Testament worship to New Testament worship became a seamless garment, not a rejection of Old Testament

GOD AND FATHER OF OUR LORD JESUS CHRIST

worship torn from the fabric of the Church, but a fulfillment and addition to the worship so common to believing Jews. They worshiped the same God, "the God and Father of our Lord Jesus Christ." Many times YHWH is referred to in this manner by the Apostles. Romans 15:6, 2 Corinthians 1:3, and Ephesians 1:3 and 17, all give praise and glory to the God and Father of our Lord Jesus Christ.

This change came in the earthly residence of YHWH's Spirit who actively and intimately led God's people in how to worship the Living God. The apostles' activities and writings became the visible model for believers to follow. The following selected encounters that the apostles experienced with YHWH God are models of praise-worship for us today.

ENCOUNTER 1. Peter, James and John experienced an amazing encounter when Jesus, by the Spirit, was transformed into his pre-existent glory (Luke 9:28-36). This event occurred during the months when Jesus withdrew from Galilee in order to give his disciples more personal attention. Scripture gives no clue as to the work or teaching content of the six days immediately before the Transfiguration. Jesus had such weighty materials to share with his disciples, and he knew that their immaturity in worship made it impossible for them to absorb and comprehend them. So Jesus led them into this mind-altering experience of seeing the glorified Christ.

ENCOUNTER 2. Paul also encountered and worshiped the Risen Lord in 2 Corinthians 12:1-10. In the previous verses Paul boasted about his sufferings for Jesus and enumerated several dozen ways in which he bore these in his own body. For Paul, these sufferings were his worship to the LORD, as he also told them in Romans 12:1-2. Paul so blended his selfless labors, his thanksgiving, praise, adoration and worship, his passion to reach the Gentile nations, that he slipped into this encounter in the "Mid-Heaven," into the presence of the Lord Jesus. And he was not quite sure if he experienced a vision of the Lord, or he actually went into Jesus' presence in heaven. Out of this worship experience, Jesus gave Paul a series of words that put steel into his backbone to weather the future sufferings Jesus had arranged for him.

ENCOUNTER 3. John's encounter with the living, resurrected Christ in Revelation 1:12-18 is an amazing demonstration of worship: "... I was in the Spirit...." John's exposition about Christ, the Word of God, in such beauteous detail shows that he knew the apostolic practice of thanks-praise-adoration worship. But to his astonishment, the Word came to him in vision-word form, not just words. He heard a loud voice, like a trumpet, and turned around to see the speaker. He saw the seven lamp stands and the "Son of Man" standing in their midst. Then John described in detail the features and clothing of the Son of Man. And he wrote down the words he heard so that believers for the rest of time would exult in their Risen Lord. And later in the book of Revelation we will look at John's magnificent encounter with Jesus and revelation of worship in the Throne Room.

> **The apostolic Worship Lifestyle: joy – ceaseless prayer – thanksgiving**

APOSTOLIC WORSHIP CHARACTERISTICS AND PRAYER LIFE.

With this challenge of the apostolic encounters with God, let's join their worship of the Living God and examine how that worship was expressed in day-to-day life. Acts 2:42-46 tells us that the Jewish Christians devoted themselves to (1) the apostles' teaching and (2) the corporate fellowship of believers in worship, and (3) the breaking of bread, probably the Lord's Supper, and to (4) prayer both private and public. Every day they continued to meet together in the Temple Courts. The Christians also broke bread in their homes, praising God and enjoying the favor of all the people. Here we find the major pattern for worshiping the Lord among the early Christians, worship patterns that believers, as businessmen, soldiers, and evangelists, carried to the full extent of the Roman Empire within a few years.

Perhaps the phrase that best summarizes the prayer-worship lifestyle of the apostolic era we find in Paul's letter to one of the first church-plants in the Greek province of Macedonia in Thessalonica. "Be joyful always...pray without ceasing...give thanks in all circumstances..." (I Thessalonians 5:16-17). The Spirit of God moved strongly among believers to build this three-aspect worship style: Joy! Prayer! Thanksgiving!

Much later, in the latter second and early third centuries, fervent believers began to move out of the cities into desert areas. They felt that their leadership had regularized Christianity by melding it with pagan cultural practices. They would no longer tolerate this compromised Christianity and went out to seek places of solitude where one could practice the worship lifestyle of prayer, praise, and thanksgiving. In turn, the believers organized themselves into communities that became forerunners of monastic orders today.

APOSTOLIC PRAYERS.

Now look at some of the most significant Pauline prayers to catch the tenor or intent of apostolic prayer-worship. Notice that after the declaration of prayer and praise, invariably the Word of God emerges with new clarity as to the dimensions of our relationship to Christ Jesus. All the Apostolic authors carry this same perspective: to live in continual worship of thanks-praise-worship. See how Paul's wording becomes for us our worship-prayer style and prayer for others. We blend our worship of the Living God with our desires for fellow believers. Worship of our God releases in us the work of the Holy Spirit so that we can comprehend the various needs of those around us and ask appropriately for their healing in spirit and body.

- EPHESIANS 1:15-23. Paul never stopped giving thanks for the Ephesian believers; he remembered their faith and love. The Spirit released to Paul this marvelous prayer for believers everywhere, that (1) God give them the Spirit of wisdom and revelation to know him better and open the eyes of their hearts to be enlightened to see (2) the hope and purpose to which God has called them; (3) the riches of the glorious inheritance already received, and (4) to experience the incomparably great power of Christ in them. He went on to describe what that life-sustaining power is for us now, like the working of his mighty strength which he exerted in Christ when he raised him from the dead and seated him at his right hand.
- EPHESIANS 3: 14-19. Paul, kneeling before the Father, prayed that God, out of his glorious riches, would (1) strengthen the believers with power through the Holy Spirit in their inner person, so that Christ might fully dwell in their hearts through faith. Then he asked that God would (2) root and establish them in love so that they might have the power to grasp the full dimensions of the love of Christ and asked that they (3) know Christ's love that surpasses human knowledge (not unknowable, but never completely known) so that they may be filled up to the measure of all the fullness of God. After these requests, in verses 20-21, Paul moved into intense worship describing the vast reality in God himself, "to do immeasurably more that all we ask or imagine according to his power that is at work within us...."
- PHILIPPIANS 1:9-11. The Philippians' partnership in the Gospel brought Paul much joy. He prayed for them with joy and trusted Jesus to carry out what he had started in them. He asked God (1) to make the love they already had to abound more and more, and (2) to fill that love with knowledge of God and depth of insight into relationship with

God. Paul wanted them (3) to be able to discern what is best, (4) be pure and blameless until Christ returns, and (5) be filled with the fruit of righteousness through Jesus Christ so that their lives become an act of worship to the glory and praise of God.

- COLOSSIANS 1:3, 9-11. Paul thanked God for the holy and faithful believers in Colosse, referring to their reputation for faith and love. He told them that he never stopped praying for them, and asked God (1) to fill them with a knowledge of his will with all wisdom and understanding given by the Spirit; that they (2) live a life worthy of the Lord's Name; (3) please him in every way; and (4) bear fruit in every good work they engage, (5) grow in their knowledge of God more fully every day, (6) be strengthened with all power by his glorious might so they have endurance and patience; and (7) that they joyfully give thanks to Father who has qualified them to share in the inheritance of the saints in the Kingdom of Light.

> **The fullness of the filial relationship complete, the complexity of YHWH Elohim breaks forth in trinitarian splendor**

FILIAL NAMES REVEALED TO THE APOSTLES OF THE NEW COVENANT. In abundance, the names of YHWH Elohim pour forth from the apostolic leaders. The spirit-anointed Word that lives in them bubbles up within their spirits and we read names of God never even imagined under the Old Covenant. Now under the fullness of the filial revelation completed, the complexity of YHWH-Elohim breaks forth in trinitarian splendor.

YHWH – THE FATHER OF OUR LORD JESUS CHRIST, THE GLORIOUS FATHER. Paul speaks of "the Father of our Lord Jesus Christ, the glorious Father" (Ephesians 1:17) and "the Father from whom all fatherhood in heaven and earth derives its name" (II Corinthians 8:6). In Colossians 1:15 and 18, Paul reveals Christ as the Image of the Invisible God....the Firstborn over all creation...the Head of the Body, the church! Peter shows us the triuneness of the Living God in the "foreknowledge of God the Father....the sanctifying work of the Spirit for obedience to Jesus Christ and sprinkling by his blood" (1 Peter 1:2). John shows us the Christ as the Word who forever lives in the presence of God, Elohim (John 1). John speaks of Jesus' various names in the "I AM" passages, culminating in his supreme expression of his own identity before the Jewish leaders: "before Abraham was born (or ever lived), I AM (that is I am YHWH)" (John 8:58) in which he declared that he is God. And throughout all the Gospels, we read the account of the Triune-appearance at Jesus' conception and his baptism: Father-Son-Spirit all present at the same moment.

YHWH – THE GOD AND FATHER OF OUR LORD JESUS CHRIST....THE GOD OF ALL GRACE. Other expressions also proclaim his names: "Praise be to the God and Father of our Lord Jesus Christ (1 Peter 1:3) and "The God of all grace, who called you to his eternal glory in Christ" (1 Peter 5:10). The writer to the Hebrews sees the Son as the radiance of his Father, the exact representation of Father's very being (Hebrews 1:3). The writer continues in this chapter to set forth the complexity of God as Father and Son and builds the basis for all the trinitarian teachings that covers the church since that date.

YHWH – THE GOD WHO GIVES ENDURANCE AND ENCOURAGEMENT....COMPASSION AND THE GOD OF ALL COMFORT. Paul says in Romans 15:5-6, May the God who gives endurance and encouragement give you the same attitude of mind toward each other that Christ Jesus had, so that with one mind and one voice you may glorify the God and Father of our Lord Jesus Christ. Similar to that is Paul's praise in 2 Corinthians 1:3: Praise be to the God and Father of our Lord Jesus Christ, the Father of compassion and the God of all comfort.

YHWH – ALPHA AND OMEGA, WHO WAS AND WHO IS AND WHO IS TO COME. John the Beloved in the Revelation brings into one book the most names for the Living God for any book in the Bible: "'I am the Alpha and the Omega' says the Lord God (YHWH Elohim), who is and who and who is to come, the Almighty" (Revelation 1:8). "...I am the First and the Last. I am the Living One; I was dead, and behold I am alive forever and ever..." (Revelation 1:17-18).

YHWH – HIM WHO... Then in Revelation 2 and 3, there are seven descriptive names of Jesus Christ at the start of each of the seven letters to the churches. The apostles practiced using the descriptive names of God. Believers from then until now have continued to hear new descriptive names for God in response to the Spirit's prompting.

- Him who holds the seven stars in his right hand and walks among the seven golden lampstands (Revelation 2:1).
- Him who is the First and the Last, who died and come to life again (Revelation 2:8).
- Him who has the sharp, double-edged sword" (Revelation 2:12).
- The words of the Son of God whose eyes are like blazing fire and whose feet are like burnished brass (Revelation 2:18).
- Him who holds the seven spirits of God (or, the sevenfold Spirit of God) and the seven stars (Revelation 3:1).
- Him who is holy and true, who holds the key of David (Revelation 3:7).
- These are the words of the Amen, the faithful and true Witness, the Ruler of God's creation (Revelation 3:14).

YHWH – KING OF KINGS AND LORD OF LORDS. John heard many other names for the Living God as he watched the worship scenario in the Throne Room with the One-who-sits-on-the-throne (Revelation 4-5). Then as history played out before John's spiritual eyes we hear his names, culminate in 19:17, revealing Jesus as the King of Kings and Lord of Lords (19:17).

WORSHIPING YHWH-JESUS-FATHER-SPIRIT WITH THE APOSTLES

The practice of thanksgiving-praise-adoration-worship prepares the believer for encountering the Living Christ in his own life experience. Such encounters are not the goal of our worship-lifestyle, but a serendipity that only God controls. If we search for an encounter with Jesus just to boast about it, we probably will never experience one. But if we pursue the Living God with a worship-lifestyle, then Jesus may just share such encounters between himself and his worshiper.

GIVE THANKS AND PRAISE. Make a list of the topics for which the apostles gave thanks and praise to Father and Jesus. Then spend time giving thanks and praising God for these things and similar things in your daily life, as did our apostolic leaders of the early church. Thank and praise God that he is holy, that he is worthy, that he is almighty, that he is eternal.

REFLECT AS YOU USE MODELS OF APOSTOLIC PRAYERS. In your own worship and prayer life, focus on thanksgiving and praise of who our God, Jesus, is. Then be drawn into the growing silence of adoration and worship. Gather your heart around the Throne of grace.

Section Six

Worshiping YHWH in this Present Age and the Age to Come

Worship of YHWH in the present age is entered through Jesus and done in the Holy Spirit. This concluding section will first delve into who YHWH is through the names and person of the Holy Spirit and then look at the revelation of YHWH in the book of Revelation as the One Who Sits on the Throne with the Lion-Lamb.

We worship the Holy Spirit in the completeness of the Father and Son

The Holy Spirit

The personhood of the Holy Spirit in the Godhead is as multifaceted as the person of the Father and the person of the Son. The Spirit "shares titles held in common by the Father and the Son; he receives these titles due to his natural and intimate relationship with them," says Basil the Great on the Holy Spirit. This is the context out of which the Names of the Holy Spirit flow.

In an attempt to express worship of the Holy Spirit, the church fathers used the term "worshiping YHWH through Jesus in the Holy Spirit." This is a direct quote from the third century. In other words, the Spirit is worshiped in terms of God the Father and God the Son. We worship the Holy Spirit in the completeness of the Father and Son. This same Holy Spirit is the one who came upon the believers in Acts 2, the same Spirit who hovered and brooded on the waters of creation in Genesis 1 and the same Spirit who hovers and broods over us.

The Holy Spirit, according to the revelation of Scripture through Jesus Christ in John 14 through 17, holds the depth of the meaning in what we call the Godhead. The word Godhead is a word created by theologians who were trying to find a term that would express the unity of God as Father, Son and Spirit. So we are given that heritage from the early church as their way of talking about God as Father-Son-Spirit in one word.

The effectiveness of the church to address the training of its family, as well as addressing society's problems and the fulfillment of the Great Commission — all these ministries depend on each believer's personal integration into the person and work of the Spirit,

> **In the age to come, worship is complete and unstoppable**

Without the Spirit's gifts and anointing, we remain like those who have begun a study program but haven't graduated and are therefore unprepared for the task. From Jesus' perspective, every worker in the vineyard must learn to depend entirely upon the person and work of the Spirit of God. Followers who do not take seriously the work and ministry of the Holy Spirit soon fall victim to the schemes of Satan and his devious ways of self-centeredness and self-deception.

Worshiping YHWH in this Present Age and the Age to Come

Him Who Sits on the Throne and The Lion-Lamb

In the age to come, worship is complete and unstoppable: Father, Son, and Spirit together around the throne. Revelation 1:8 begins by declaring his name as the Alpha and Omega, who is, and who was and who is to come, the Almighty! The Son is among the seven golden lamp stands, standing "like a son of man" in Revelation 1:13.

Then in John's revelation of heaven he sees Father on the throne. In chapter four, the four Living creatures start off with their worship with, "Holy, holy is the Lord God Almighty, who was, and is, and is to come." They gave glory, honor and thanks and were joined by the twenty-four elders who declared to him who sits on the throne…and lives forever and ever. They then lay down their crowns and declare his worthiness, "You are worthy, our Lord and God, to receive glory and honor and power, for you created all things, and by your will they were created and have their being" (Revelation 4;11).

Revelation 5:6 follows with Jesus as the Lamb standing in the center of the throne. Here the four living creatures and the elders sing a new song of the Lamb's worthiness to take the scroll and open its seals. They were then joined by angels and every living creature to give him praise and honor and glory and power, forever and ever. You are invited to join this anthem of praise there too even now!

Worship continues throughout the entire book of Revelation as we watch history being played out. In triumph, we see Jesus as the Rider on the white horse who is called Faithful and True. "He is dressed in a robe dipped in blood, and his name is The Word of God …. And on his robe and on his thigh he has this name written: KING OF KINGS AND LORD OF LORDS. (Revelation 19:11-16). Worship him!

In the final summation of names in Revelation 22:12-16, Jesus reveals himself as the Alpha and Omega, the First and Last, the Beginning and the End. He says "I AM the Root and Offspring of David, the bright Morning Star." The Spirit and the bride say, "'Come!' Whoever is thirsty, let him come; and whoever wishes, let him take the free gift of the water life." Come and worship!

Chapter Twelve

WORSHIPING YHWH THROUGH JESUS IN THE HOLY SPIRIT

In the study of the Holy Spirit we freely admit that we step into a mystery that has not been fully delineated in the Scripture. This is the most likely reason why the church fathers in the early centuries did not make hard and fast conclusions about the Holy Spirit as they did about God the Father and God the Son. God the Father is extensively revealed through the entire Old Testament, and then finally through Jesus the Son who revealed a fullness of the Father that is never gathered from the Old Testament. But nothing in Scripture describes the Holy Spirit apart from Jesus and Father. In the New Testament, there are many references to worshiping God as God and worshiping Jesus Christ as Jesus Christ. But this third area of worshiping the Holy Spirit, the text is strangely quiet.

Yet we see in the first moment of the incarnation that the Holy Spirit was in complete oneness with the Godhead. Luke 1:35 tells us that Father, Son and Holy Spirit were all present and working together: "The angel answered, "The **Holy Spirit** will come upon you, and the power of the **Most High** will overshadow you, so the holy one to be born will be called the **Son of God**."

ENCOUNTERING THE HOLY SPIRIT THROUGH HIS NAMES

Revealed extensively by Jesus Christ, the Holy Spirit, out of his own deity and commission by Father, lives within us and makes it his purpose to reveal to us individually who he is. It's like the Holy Spirit has willingly given himself equally among all the members of the body who follow Jesus Christ. And that individual touch of the Holy Spirit in you and in me, that's the point of mystery. The Spirit of God will reveal things about himself to you that he will not reveal to me or other believers. That intimacy of the Holy Spirit with the individual follower of Christ, that is deliberate. That is Father's purpose and is the purpose of Jesus Christ.

I would guess that the individuality of the Spirit's work within us is the crowning gift of Jesus to the church. Father planned this, Jesus paid the price for it and the Spirit makes himself known to us individually. It is an entirely accurate and trustworthy description of the nature of the Holy Spirit that gives us a myriad of applications of the Holy Spirit in our lives. This is like a garden full of innumerable plants and flowers, some that we know and some that look quite strange to us. So this is the garden of our labor, to come to know who the Holy Spirit is in his holiness as well as how his holiness takes root in our natures and produces its own garden.

Now let's look at how the disciples encountered the Holy Spirit through his self-revealed names. In John chapters 14-17, Jesus revealed to the disciples the unique names that best describe who the Holy Spirit is. This passage is the greatest expression of the work of the Holy Spirit in the entire Scripture. Jesus has given us a series of names and descriptors about who the Holy Spirit is and what he does. For each of us, these names will become a lifelong goal of study, of searching, of developing a deep sensitivity to what Jesus has said about the Spirit since they are from the mouth of Jesus and comprise the very word of God.

THE HOLY SPIRIT IS COUNSELOR. Jesus described the Spirit, the Counselor, in John 14:16-17: "And I will ask the Father, and he will give you another Counselor to be with you forever—the

Spirit of truth. Here John makes several assertions about the name, character and nature of the Holy Spirit."

- The Spirit's source as Counselor is in Father. Later, the text says that the Spirit proceeds from the Father. He steps forth from him as the essence of Father's nature. The Counselor comes from and goes out from the Father. This locates the origin of the Spirit within Father. So the Father releases the Spirit at Jesus' command.
- The Spirit will be another Counselor. Jesus' work of counseling and mentoring the disciples will be picked up, continued and culminated in the person and work of the Holy Spirit. The Spirit effectively replaces Jesus' work of initiating the church. The Spirit carries on Jesus' work throughout the days of the church on earth and then will take her into heaven's realms where he continues his work of nurturing and counseling the church.

> **The translation "counselor" clarifies the Spirit's work as helper to all who belong to Christ**

- The Holy Spirit-Counselor will live in the disciples forever as the Spirit of Truth. The Holy Spirit-Counselor will live in them both in time and after death in eternity. The Holy Spirit steps out of Father's presence into your life and what he brings is holiness.

Reflect for a moment on the Holiness of the Spirit's Counsel. Since the Spirit is holy through and through, all his counsel comes to us in that mode of total holiness. Therefore, since his counsel is always holy and true, then our goal is to develop our knowledge and understanding of him who is both holy and true.

You might ask, just why use the term "Counselor," rather than the older term "Comforter"? That's a good question because it takes us to the heart of the Spirit's activity here on earth. By naming the Holy Spirit the "Comforter," the 16th century translators unwittingly limited his activity to that of comforting those in sufferings, as in 2 Corinthians 1:3-11 where Paul's description of the Spirit's work is in affording comfort. But the Greek term, *"paraclete,"* of the first century AD, had a much broader meaning in Greek. An excellent paraphrase of the meaning of *"paraclete"* would be "the one called alongside to help." Thus the translation "Counselor" more fully explains the Spirit's work in the task as a helper, one who comes to the aid of all those who belong to Christ.

THE HOLY SPIRIT IS TEACHER. Jesus' names the Spirit as the Teacher in John 14:26: But the Counselor, the Holy Spirit, whom the Father will send in my name, will teach you all things and will remind you of everything I have said to you.

Jesus continues with his instruction about the Teacher-Spirit and how he works to teach the disciples all things. He promises that the Spirit will also remind them of everything that Jesus had previously taught them. The Spirit will go on teaching them all things yet unsaid. This promise alone should have quieted the disciples' hearts. But more than that, Jesus gave this astounding assurance that the Spirit will go on reminding them about Jesus' words, those that perhaps they had forgotten, due to unbelief, lack of attention, or just plain forgetfulness. The Spirit as Teacher works with us to unlock and unpack the meaning of the teachings of Jesus. We can trust the Spirit as Teacher to remind us of biblical truth that has slipped our minds. The effectiveness of the church to address the training of its family, as well as addressing society's problems and the fulfillment of the Great Commission—all these ministries depend on each believer's personal integration into the person and work of the Spirit,

Without the Spirit's gifts and anointing, we remain like those who have begun a study program but haven't graduated and are therefore unprepared for the task. From Jesus' perspective, every worker in the vineyard must learn to depend entirely upon the person and work of the Spirit of God. Followers who do not take seriously the work and ministry of the Holy Spirit soon fall victim to the schemes of Satan and his devious ways of self-centeredness and self-deception.

> **The closer we are to Jesus the more we are subject to the direct intrusion and instruction of the Holy Spirit; and the more unpredictable every day becomes**

We also know from Paul's writings, in Romans 12, I Corinthians 12, and Ephesians 4 that the Spirit of God distributes many gifts, one of which is teaching. Paul himself is a fine example of the apostolic teacher. Each writer who contributed to the New Testament carried within him this teaching gift. This gift has as its major function the unpacking and explanation of the truths from the life and words of Jesus. As Jesus continuously exhorted his disciples to speak his words and do his works, so also that injunction continues for us today, to continue teaching even as he taught us and to continue in the works that demonstrate his teaching.

As we know, the Spirit of God lives and works outside our space-time universe. He chooses to intersect with us through our daily experience on earth at his pleasure—often without any warning. He assumes the right to intrude upon our daily schedule to teach us, confront and direct us. The closer a believer comes to Jesus, the more he or she is subject to the direct intrusion and instruction of the Holy Spirit, and therefore the more unpredictable every day becomes.

THE HOLY SPIRIT IS THE ONE WHO TESTIFIES ABOUT JESUS. John 15:26 is anther verse that guides our faith and thinking about the Holy Spirit—the One who gives testimony or witness about Jesus: "When the Counselor comes, whom I will send to you from the Father, the Spirit of truth, who goes out from the Father, he will testify about me. And you also must testify, for you have been with me from the beginning."

> **Our witness, generated and protected by the Holy Spirit, carries the freshness of heaven itself**

John 15:26 focuses on the meaning of the term "testify." In Greek, *marturew* means to be a witness, to attest, bear witness or testify. In Greek culture, the word carried the idea of giving testimony in legal situations, under the careful eye of the presiding judge. The Jewish Torah and culture filled this term with meaning far beyond that of the Greek legal system of the first century AD. But in the Hebrew approach, the rabbis, especially the chief priest, could when appropriate force a practicing Jew to swear by the person of YHWH that what he was saying was in fact true. The Jew had to be aware that he was testifying in YHWH's presence, that what the Jew was speaking had the same ring of truth as those words would carry if YHWH himself were speaking those words.

The Counselor, the Spirit of Truth, now comes wrapped in an injunction for Jesus' disciples and all who follow in their footsteps. Through the Holy Spirit, we too are given the work of testifying to, and bearing witness about, Jesus the Christ, his person and his work. We the followers of Christ are to continue the work and words of Jesus.

The truth that the Paraclete-Counselor communicates to us also carries the holiness that characterizes the Holy Spirit. So every witness that the Spirit gives us to convey to others comes with the holiness of God the Father. For the words themselves—sourced in Father through the Spirit—carry the holiness inherent in each Person of the trinity. Reflect for a moment on the sacredness of our witness, our testimony about Jesus Christ, whether in teaching, in personal witness, in daily occupation or in family. Our witness, generated and protected by the Holy Spirit, carries the freshness of heaven itself. From the depths of Father's purposes, as interpreted and carried by the Holy Spirit, our witness about Christ has within it a truthfulness and holiness that characterizes the Holy Spirit himself. The ideas and words sourced in the Holy Spirit come to us with all his inherent truthfulness and holiness that the Spirit lives in. This is the ministry of the blessed Holy Spirit as he inhabits our mind-soul-body-spirit on our pilgrim's journey towards Father's ultimate presence and glory.

THE HOLY SPIRIT IS THE ONE WHO CONVICTS Jesus names the Spirit as the One Who Convicts in John 16:7-11: "Unless I go away, the Counselor will not come to you; but if I go, I will send him to you. When he comes, he will convict the world of guilt in regard to sin and righteousness and judgment:

- In regard to sin, because men do not believe in me;
- In regard to righteousness, because I am going to the Father, where you can see me no longer;
- In regard to judgment, because the prince of this world now stands condemned. "

Jesus' promise of the Holy Spirit's work to convict covers in depth the area of sin. The Spirit of God has access to all people, and Father has commissioned him to convince and convict people—worldwide—as to their own individual disobedience to Father's truth, revealed first in the "law written on the heart." When we wander and disobey the law of God written indelibly on the heart, the Spirit begins to remind us of our offence towards the Father of all humanity and is there to warn us, to correct us; then, when ignored, to convict us and bring us to the point of repenting before Father for offending him in our thoughts and activities. And the Spirit conveys to the repentant one both forgiveness and cleansing that flow from Father's presence.

Specifically, the Spirit works with all people on earth to remind, convince and convict us about sin, as offense against God the Father; about righteousness, that which characterizes Father and Son and that we lack entirely; and about judgment, the incredible punishment that awaits those who refuse to acknowledge the Spirit's work and who refuse to yield.

The idea of conviction includes individual conscience as well as codified laws of moral behavior. Both aspects, as well as every type of moral injunction in between conscience and laws fall under the general activity of the Holy Spirit as he speaks directly to the conscience of every human on earth. People may heed the gentle nudge of the Spirit or ignore his insistent injunctions in local society. Nevertheless, the Spirit of God carries out the attitudes and standards of God the Father, whom the Spirit represents and from whom the Spirit strides forth to carry out his work.

The Calvary event marked the end of the era of unatoned sin for earth's populations. Father's rescue plan, on one hand, effectively wiped out any hindrance for anyone on earth to access Father's presence: Jesus paid for the sin of all people in all ages. On the other hand, Father completed this rescue plan by dispatching the Holy Spirit worldwide to convince people of Father's presence and his totally righteous standards to which all may attain through the righteous life and death of our Savior.

THE HOLY SPIRIT IS THE SPIRIT OF TRUTH. In John 16:13, Jesus names the Holy Spirit "the Spirit of Truth." In John 8:44, Jesus characterized Satan as a liar and father of lies. In contrast in these verses, Jesus characterized the Holy Spirit as the Spirit of Truth. Therefore at every point of Jesus' life and work, Jesus spoke truth: truth as measured by true words Father had given Jesus to teach. This work the Spirit continues today.

John's detailed portrayal of the Spirit's person and activity as Truth complete his revelation of the names of the Holy Spirit. John continues quoting Jesus directly in 16:12-15:

- I have much more to say to you, more than you can now bear. But when he, the Spirit of truth, comes, he will guide you into all truth.
- He will not speak on his own; he will speak only what he hears, and he will tell you what is yet to come.
- He will bring glory to me by taking what is mine and making it known to you.
- All that belongs to the Father is mine. That is why I said that the Spirit will take from what is mine and make it known to you.

Within this short passage, John shares with us two different activities of the Holy Spirit as truth, 1) that of guiding us into Jesus' words, and 2) that of glorifying Christ and his life and work. Jesus wanted to fill the hearts and minds of his disciples, but they could not absorb any more at this time. So Jesus addressed that issue of "too much, too soon." We surmise that the disciples agreed in their hearts, since the startling activities of the previous twelve hours in Passover week had shocked all of them: his triumphal entry, his prediction of his coming death, his washing of the disciples' feet and his prediction of betrayal by Judas and of denial by Peter. Jesus did not wish to contribute to more overload, so he described what would happen to and in them when the Holy Spirit had actually arrived.

Jesus said that the Spirit will guide us into all truth, all the truth that we need at any one time for any one situation. The Spirit will guide us by releasing to us the truth that comes through Jesus, the truth that is appropriate for each given challenge. Jesus does not refer to philosophic truth that the world's thinkers have developed over the centuries. Jesus referred to the truths that revealed and displayed Father's eternal purposes, the truths that are needed to resolve life's problems.

> Jesus did not refer to philosophic truths but to the truths that revealed father's eternal purposes: truths we need to resolve life's problems today

The Holy Spirit Is One Who Authenticates Father's Nature. The Counselor as the Spirit of Truth, comes from the depths of Father's being and presence, the very depths of God's truth. Therefore whatever the Spirit says or teaches or witnesses comes with the full authentication of Father's nature, the nature which is truth. The Spirit's work in us is so penetrating that gradually our spirits become individual "spirits of truth," because the Spirit's truth has reformed, reformatted, and filled individual human spirits with his very life.

Worshiping YHWH through Jesus in the Holy Spirit

This phrase, "worship YHWH through Jesus in the Holy Spirit," came to be normative in the expression of God in his triunity. Admittedly, for any of us to try to embrace God in his triunity in any one moment in time is simply impossible. So we want to touch him through specific words that Jesus has introduced to us that guide us in our practice of worship throughout the day, every day.

YIELD. The first word of worship is that of yield. When we start studying God in his triunity, we start at this point. There's no way to embrace God with our finite minds that are structured for time-space universe. We understand that YHWH, Jesus, and the Holy Spirit are from outside our time-space universe and dip in and out as they will. Remember, God in his triunity is caring for at least two billion followers today worldwide. So the enormity of who God is as YHWH, Jesus, the Holy Spirit, far outweighs the enormity of our universe. That kind of information is reserved for us when we get into Father's Presence in Heaven.

There's something else about yielding reserved for us who are incarnate. That is, we come to earth in bodies and there's something about the body that God appreciates and blesses so deeply. He wants to hear from us in our human flesh and blood forms. Angels do not have what we have. Their bodies are pure spirit. But what we are, created in the Image of God and designed to be able to yield to the Spirit and do our work at the same time. You say, that sounds impossible. Ask God. Start by yielding to him and learning to develop a pattern of yielding, giving thanks, praising, adoring, and waiting to hear his voice. Let it develop in your daily life. The goal of what Father's after is to be fully employed in your body and soul and also to be worshiping in your spirit.

GIVE THANKS. As he gives us a sense of yieldedness, then we can enter into giving thanks. So the first response of the believer in sensing the Presence of God is to simply say thank you, thank you, thank you. Elaborate on thank you with as many more words as you can think of. Keep on thanking and thanking and thanking.

PRAISE. For the believer to praise his Maker is a natural flow of thanksgiving. This praise that we give to Father, Son, and Spirit can also be expressed with words and names from Exodus 34:5-7 where YHWH expresses the essence of his person in the form of seven names. Praise him with these names. He is the one who is grace personified. His Spirit is compassion personified. His Spirit is the personification of covenant love; that is, loving kindness. His Spirit is the personification of faithfulness. That's his name, that's his character, that's who he is in his essence and that's who we are becoming as Father through the Spirit conforms us to the Image of Christ.

ADORATION. Praise may be momentary, if not spontaneous, but adoration is focused and deliberate over a period of time. Again, we can adore Father, Son, and Spirit with his self-revealed names. Adoration is not something that we can rush into. Rather, in God's presence we pause, and we take time and talk with the Father, and with the Son, and with the Spirit, with praise, but going a step further into concentrated praise which then becomes adoration.

WORSHIP, WAIT AND LISTEN FOR HIM TO SHARE HIS HEART. This is a very personal experience for each of us as we approach the Lord to worship Father, Son and Holy Spirit. We worship in the sense of waiting, of pausing. There are three favorite words that the desert fathers and mothers developed over the centuries and they are: silence, solitude, and waiting. This is the process by which we attempt to quiet our own soul while we are busily involved in the work that God has given us. But there is a quietness that comes into our spirit, which is our spirit's response to the Presence of God. In that quietness we cease from all striving and initiating with our own will. We are able to wait that he might share his presence.

REST. YHWH's presence means Rest. The last stage in worship is when God himself came and rested. He rested because everything was already purposed, declared and set in motion. This is something you do and it's between you and your God. You rest in his completeness. This automatically prevents worry, fretting, overdoing things; in other words, driving yourself too much. This quiets everything in a supernatural way and at the same time imparts the assurance that it's already done. Now you are ready to do his will and work, and speak his words of life.

My prayer is that God would accompany you, move close to you, and let you touch his presence in such a way that he facilitates your worship. To him be the glory, and the honor and the power through Jesus Christ our Lord. Amen.

Chapter Thirteen

WORSHIPING YHWH, THE ONE-WHO-SITS-ON-THE-THRONE

After the risen Christ delivered his letters to the seven churches, John saw a Spirit-generated vision of a door standing open in heaven (Revelation 4:1). He again heard a loud voice like the trumpet sound of Revelation 1:10, that commanded him to move upwards and through the door so that the LORD could show him what must happen after this. The Spirit swept John up and into the very throne room of YHWH Elohim El Shaddai. John found himself at the center point and passion of all existence, at the very source of all that exists in heaven and earth. What Father wants us to see is just this-the reality of what is going on in Heaven now and in the age to come.

> **All worship is a response to all that is emanating from the Throne**

ENCOUNTERING YHWH, THE ONE-WHO-SITS-ON-THE-THRONE

All worship is a response to all that is emanating from the throne. The throne room is full of holy worship. John the Beloved saw the vision from the throne room and walked, unexpectedly, into full-orbed worship of the Living God by all present. He described in John 4 who and what he saw in vivid details.

Worshiping YHWH, the One-Who-Sits-On-The-Throne

Activities, Sights and Dramatis Personae in the Throne Room.

1. The first thing John saw in heaven was **a throne with a personage sitting on it**. He was unable to name the person so he began to describe him indirectly, by comparisons. In the inadequacy of his human language, he described this exalted personage in terms of the reflected brilliance of precious stones: the One-who-sits-on–the-throne has the appearance of jasper (it can be green, red or purple) and carnelian (reddish in appearance). John saw the One-who-sits-on–the-throne, never identified by any other name, but who was the focal point of all worship.
2. **Encircling the throne, John saw a rainbow** and described it as resembling an emerald, perhaps a greenish hue somehow reflected in ALL the colors of the rainbow. Some commentators explain the color and noise as the expression of the Almighty YHWH without a translation factor. He takes the reality of YHWH himself and put him in images that we humans can comprehend. The culmination is described in Colossians 1:15 when Paul spoke of Jesus of Nazareth as the visible expression of the invisible God.
3. Next John saw **24 thrones that surround the throne and the twenty-four elders**, wearing gold crowns and clothed in white garments.
4. Then from the throne he saw and heard **flashes of lightning, rumblings and peals of thunder**. Some have suggested that the lightning, rumblings and thunder are the speaking of the Eternal Son of God, the expressive Word of God, in his pre-incarnated state, that is, without a human body. If these sounds speak of the Son of God, the Word, then the blazing lamps might well speak of the Spirit's presence before the throne.
5. Then he saw **seven blazing lamps**. These were the seven spirits of God, or the seven-fold spirit of God, who in some way

beyond our imagination orchestrates and manages this worship scenario.

6. John also saw **a sea of glass before the throne**, like a sea of clear crystal. Exodus 24:10 and Ezekiel 1:22 described similar sights. Ezekiel says that they were "sparkling like ice, and awesome."

7. Last John saw **four living creatures positioned around the throne,** in the center of the throne room. The first living creature looked like a lion; the second living creature looked like an ox; the third living creature looked like he has the face of a man; and the fourth living creature looked like a flying eagle. John further describes each living creature as having six wings and again mentions that each creature has eyes everywhere, even under their wings. Apparently, they see and know everything taking place everywhere. While Isaiah saw the seraphim in continual activity, worshiping and serving YHWH (Isaiah 6:1-5), Ezekiel saw them as ready, instantly available, to "go wherever the Spirit would go," to serve YHWH's purposes in the universe (Ezekiel 1:4-28).

WORSHIP AROUND THE THRONE. John then recorded two worship proclamation songs directed to the One-who-sits-on–the-throne.

1. In the first proclamation song, he hears the four living creatures address the One-who-sits-on–the-throne. They never stop saying day and night, **"Holy, Holy, Holy is the Lord God Almighty, Who was, and is and is to come"** (Revelation 4:8). They focus on the holiness, the sovereignty and the eternality of God.

2. Whenever the four living creatures give glory, honor and thanks to the One-who-sits-on–the-throne and who lives forever and ever, the twenty-four elders lay down their crowns and proclaim to all heaven the second of the heavenly adorations, the first one of worthiness, saying, **"You are worthy, our Lord and God, to receive glory**

and honor and power, for you created all things and by your will they were created and have their being" (Revelation 4:11). They emphasize the worthiness of God to receive glory, honor and power, because of his chosen created order. His created order gives us our very being and expresses his glory, honor, and power.

With this worship of his worthiness are two characteristics of the One-who-sits-on–the-throne. First, that he is worthy above all to receive glory, honor and power. Second, he alone created all things for his own purposes. For that reason all things exist. By him, and with the help of no one else, all things exist. The very creation that came from his fingers now brings to him all glory, honor, and power.

Names Used in Unceasing Worship of YHWH, the One-Who-Sits-On–The-Throne

John saw the living creatures in worship, their first and only activity. In their worship the four living creatures and the elders recognize the two greatest characteristics about YHWH: his holiness and his eternality. Their endless worship fills heaven with songs of holiness and reveal these names exalting him.

> **Our hearts yearn to join the creatures' everlasting chorus**

The Lord God Almighty, who was, and is and is to come. As the four living creatures incessantly worship YHWH, they recognize his holy name (Revelation 4:8). Day and night they never stop declaring the holiness of the Lord God Almighty, El Shaddai, Who was and is and is to come..

Him Who-sits-on-the-throne and Who-lives-forever-and-ever. These two names are encountered in verse 9.

They summarize the whole scene and focus, "giving glory, honor and thanks" to YHWH on the throne. John describes the elders' response to YHWH that every time the living creatures give glory, honor, and thanks to him who sits on the throne, then the twenty four elders also fall down before him and join in worshiping him Who-lives-forever-and-forever. When they all join in worship together, incessantly worshiping YHWH in this manner, heaven erupts in songs of praise to this YHWH.

We, too, fall down in awesome worship of him who-sits-on-the-throne. Our hearts yearn to join in the creatures' everlasting chorus to extol and adore this One whom all heaven worships.

Worshiping YHWH Together Around the Throne

Meditate. Meditate on what's happening in heaven right now to build an inner appreciation of him who sits on the throne. These awesome creatures were created for specific purposes within YHWH's sovereign rule in heaven. Heaven's worship begins here: the holiness and worthiness of YHWH.

Reflect. Reflect on these the worship elements in John's progressive disclosure of the heavenly scenario:

- The authority and eternality of the One-who-sits-on–the-throne.
- The rainbow, colors, sounds, and shapes that surround them.
- The lightning, rumblings and thunder.
- Seven lamps that were the seven-fold Spirit of God.
- The crystal sea before the throne.
- The four living creatures, like a lion, ox, man, and eagle incessantly worshipping YHWH for his holiness.
- The prostrate twenty-four elders in white, with gold crowns, surrounding the throne, worshiping YHWH for his worthiness.

WORSHIPING YHWH, THE ONE-WHO-SITS-ON-THE-THRONE

- Unceasing worship of the One-who-sits-on–the-throne.

MEMORIZE. Read over and memorize the proclamations and songs of holiness and worthiness until you have them written on your heart. That way you can speak without interruption to YHWH about his holiness and worthiness. You can also sing and share with YHWH at any time. Present the two songs to him who sits on the throne, first in thanksgiving, then in praise. Declare each detail of each song to the LORD. As his Presence grows stronger in your awareness, move towards silence before him.

WORSHIP AND ADORE. Just wait in silence in his Presence. You are in the throne room of YHWH ELOHIM, EL SHADDAI, the Source of all that exists, ground zero of all activity in Heaven and on earth. Permit him to enjoy you as his own child. And for you, just enjoy him and the privilege of being in his presence.

Chapter Fourteen

WORSHIPING YHWH, THE LION-LAMB

Like every believer since the days of John the Beloved, we stand in wonder at this One-who-sits-on-the-throne. We assume this is Father, Jesus' God and Father, but he is not identified beyond his descriptive title. Yet the entire population of heaven, numbering in the millions of millions centers on him and the unfolding revelation of the Lion-Lamb. By his sacrificial work on the cross, among covenant people and Gentiles, he demonstrated his inherent worthiness, a worthiness based on his poured-out life blood. This resulted in a redeemed people who constitute both YHWH's kingdom and who serve YHWH as his priests on earth. Together with the Lamb we all will rule on earth as kingdom-priests.

Together with the Lamb we will rule on earth as kingdom priests

ENCOUNTERING AND WORSHIPING YHWH, THE LION-LAMB

The situation in chapter 5 parallels that of chapter 4. John continues his description of the throne room, the personages and activities of the eternal worship temple. Hebrews 8:2 calls the heavenly temple, "the true tabernacle set up by the LORD, not by man." Into this temple all believers approach the Living God through the blood sacrifice of his One and Only Son, Jesus. So what John now saw was the next revelation that culminated in full-orbed worship in the heavenly temple of him who sits on the throne and to the Lamb who was slain.

THE SCROLL: GOD'S REDEMPTIVE PLAN. Then John's attention focused on the One-who-sits-on-the-throne and saw that he had a scroll in his right hand, a scroll with writing on both sides of the papyrus, sealed with seven seals. The seals show absolute authority that cannot be breached or desecrated.

Then, Revelation 4:2, a mighty angel with a mighty voice proclaimed to all inhabitants of heaven and earth, "Who is worthy to break the seals and open the scroll?" Perhaps we have here a rhetorical question that could be restated as, "There is no one worthy to break the seals and open the scroll." And quite literally, no one in all heaven and earth volunteered to step up to break the seals—because no created being had the requisite holiness, the eternity, the worthiness, and creator's role. They could not open the scroll or even look inside it.

In response, John broke into intense weeping over his disappointment that no one could be found who had the necessary prerequisites. But an elder broke in on John's grievous perplexity with a preemptory directive: "John, stop weeping! And look over there!" John heard the immortal words to look and see the uncreated Lion who springs from the tribe of Judah! But when John turned to catch a glimpse of the Lion of the tribe of Judah, the Root of David, announced by the elder, instead he saw a Lamb that looked as if it had been slain. The Lamb himself has the prerequisites to open the scroll and break its seven seals!

> **Jesus puts a human face on the immortal, invisible God who lives in unapproachable light**

Now the Lion-Lamb stepped up to the One who sat on the throne, and took the scroll of YHWH's purposes out of his right hand. In doing this, the Lion-Lamb inaugurated a new phase of YHWH's eternal purposes for redeemed mankind. Jesus, the Lion-Lamb, had within his own hand the scroll that was released to him personally based on his sacrificial life for all sinners. Now Jesus puts a human face to the immortal, invisible God who lives in unapproachable light. Jesus can now carry out, on the plane of human activity, all that Father has had in his heart from all eternity and so we next see the unfolding of time in people and song.

ACTIVITIES, SIGHTS AND DRAMATIS PERSONAE IN THE THRONE ROOM.

1. John first sees **the scroll** in the right hand of **him who sat on the throne.** George Ladd calls the scroll, "God's redemptive plan for the denouement of human history, the overthrow of evil and the gathering of a redeemed people to enjoy the blessings of God's rule" (George Eldon Ladd, *A Commentary on the Revelation of John*). This scroll held the attention of all within the throne room.
2. Next a **mighty angel** asked the question of worthiness to open the scroll. John, weeping, is asked to behold the Lion of the tribe of Judah, the Root of David.
3. Instead, John sees a Lamb, looking as if it had been slain, standing in the center of the throne, not around it or by its side! The **Lamb is in the center of the throne and had seven horns and seven eyes, which are the seven spirits of God** sent out into all the earth. It is the Lamb, not the Lion, that is in the center of the throne.
4. John then watched the **four Living creatures and the elders** fall down in worship before the Lion-Lamb. Each one of the Creatures and Elders holds a harp for worship and in their hands golden bowls full of incense—the incense that represents the prayers of all believers of all time. They sang **a new song to the Lamb** exclaiming the reasons for his worthiness

to take the scroll. This singing exalts the Lamb who is worthy of YHWH's attributes! This emphasizes that the Lion-Lamb merits the same attributes and worship given to the One-who-sits-on-the-throne.
5. John amazingly saw and heard **numberless angels** who joined the living creatures and elders to sing another song in a loud voice to the Lion-Lamb. The angels began **the next worship song**, another song to the Lamb for his worthiness.
6. But the joyous activities don't stop there. John heard **a vast, unimaginable crowd. Every created being in heaven and on earth, under the earth, on the sea – and all that is in the heaven, earth and sea – everything that exists within these spheres** – together with the living creatures and elders and angels, sing to the One-who-sits-on-the-throne and to the Lamb. Altogether, they acknowledge the deity of both the One-who-sits-on-the-throne and the Lion-Lamb. Both are worthy to receive all the attributes of God.
7. Then the four living creatures cry out their approval: **Amen!** And the twenty-four elders **fall down and worship**.

Worship Around the Throne.

John heard and recorded three more songs, the first two directed to the Lamb and the final one to both him who sits on the throne and to the Lamb.

1. **The New Song of Worship to the Lamb.** As soon as the Lion-Lamb took the scroll, John watched the four creatures with elders, worshipers and the twenty-four elders fall down in worship before the Lion-Lamb. They began a New Song, a worship chorus to the Lion-Lamb and his worthiness to take the scroll: **You are worthy to take the scroll and to open its seals, because you were slain and you purchased with your own blood people for YHWH, people from every tribe, language, people and nation. You made these purchased-people to be a king-**

dom, and to be priests to serve our God Elohim, and these purchased-people will reign on earth** (Revelation 5: 9-10).
2. **The Worthiness Chorus of Heaven: Angeles, Living Creatures and Elders.** In the next song, John heard and saw the living creatures and elders joined by a myriad of angels to sing in a loud voice the worthiness of the Lamb for his sacrificial work on Calvary: **Worthy is the Lamb who was slain to receive power and wealth, wisdom and strength, honor, glory and praise!** (Revelation 5: 12)

> **There is a current and eternal worship service that has been in session since before any human could imagine**

3. **All Creation Worships!** In the last song, John heard all the dramatis personae of the heavenly Tabernacle engage their respective roles for an extended, fuller and more intense worship of the Living God, together singing to him who sits on the throne and to the resurrected, exalted Lord Jesus Christ. Altogether, they acknowledge the deity of both the One who sits on the throne and the Lion-Lamb. Both are worthy to receive all the attributes of God: **To him who sits on the throne and to the Lamb, be praise and honor and glory and power forever and ever.** (Revelation 5: 12)

This is the current and eternal worship service that has been in session since before any human could imagine. It is no wonder that those believers with their leaders of the early church and throughout the ages have discovered patterns of worship in these five worship songs. May all God's people today discover anew these biblical songs for worshiping the Living God, the One-who-sits-on-the-throne and the Lion-Lamb.

Worshiping YHWH, the Lion-Lamb

The New Name for YHWH: The Lion-Lamb Arises

The Lion-Lamb. So to our knowledge of God's names, we add the Lion-Lamb! This is **The Lamb Who was Slain**. He has on his person seven horns representing all authority and seven eyes for all knowledge. In fact, his seven eyes are the seven spirits of God, also known as the seven-fold Spirit of God that he sends into all the earth to know everything that happens, everywhere, all the time. What the elder called the Lion, John perceived as a sacrificial Lamb, very much like the perfect lamb sacrificed each year whose blood the High Priest took into the Holy of Holies. This juxtaposition of unexpected opposites still baffles us today. How is it possible to call one and the same person both a Lion and a Lamb at the same time? Yet this Lion-Lamb stands in the center of the throne, not around it, or by its side. The Lion-Lamb stands encircled by the Living creatures and all the elders.

The Lion of the Tribe of Judah and the Root of David. Jesus' earthly lineage is joined to his heavenly, eternal personage. John heard the immortal words to look and see the Uncreated Lion who springs from the tribe of Judah. He is the Root of David. This King-Procreator has triumphed! He has won the war!

Worshiping YHWH and the Lamb Together Around the Throne

Reflect and Memorize. Bring together all five worship songs and reflect on each person and event in chapters four and five of Revelation. Memorize the five songs and prepare your heart to worship with all five songs. These five songs of worship are key and resonate throughout the book of Revelation in 7:12, 11:15-17, 15:3-4 and end with the Hallelujah song in chapter 19.

1. The Song of Holiness before YHWH (Revelation 4:8)
2. The Song of Worthiness to YHWH (4:11)

3. The New Song of the Lamb's Worthiness to take and open the scroll (5:9-10)
4. The Song of the Lamb's Worthiness of YHWH'S Attributes (5:12)
5. The Song of The Worthiness of the One-who-sits-on–the-throne and the Lion-Lamb (5:13)

GIVE THANKS AND PRAISE. Present each of these five songs to the LORD with thanksgiving for all that that together constitute the throne room scene. Thank YHWH that he created and revealed this scenario so we might worship him in the reality of who he is, not who we think he is. Praise YHWH that he is the Authority, the Eternal One, the Worthy One, the Creator. Praise YHWH for showing us the qualities of his person, his virtues, the components of his very nature, so that we might worship him in the reality of his person and view of himself, not with our limited attempts to describe who he is. Declare each song in Revelation 4 and 5 to the Lord, first in thanksgiving, then in praise.

ENTER AND WORSHIP. Wait in silence, in his presence, for the tangible presence of the One who sits on the throne, the One who created you and gave his life for you, YHWH Elohim and Jesus the Lion-Lamb. You are in the throne room of YHWH Elohim, El Shaddai, the Source of all that exists, axis of all activity in heaven and on earth. In the quietness of waiting, he overwhelms all our imperfections with his perfection, all our strivings with his might, all our questions with his wisdom, all our needs with his abundance, all our offenses with his goodness and forgiveness, all our failures with his authority, eternity, worthiness, and new creation.

EXPRESS YOUR ADORATION. ADORE. Adore the One-who-sits-on–the-throne, and the Lion-Lamb. The Spirit initiates and maintains this praise, worship, and adoration. He lives within you day and night to lift these incessant songs through your heart, mind, soul, and voice. Amen and Amen!! YHWH Elohim, El

Shaddai, him who sits on the throne, together with the Lamb looking as if it had been slain, are the object of worship by every creature in heaven and on earth and under the earth and on the sea, and all that is in them, singing praise, honor, glory and power forever and ever!

Appendices

Summary of God's Self-Revealed Names

"If I Tell You My Name, You Know Who I AM"

1. ELOHIM: Creation, Genesis 1

God, who pre-existed before and apart from our universe, creates and authors all of life from his existence and is the sheer power behind all of life. Elohim is spirit, has total power and unlimited resources. He has life in himself, and makes covenant with all creation.

2. YHWH ELOHIM: Adam, Genesis 2

The LORD God who offers relationship to all is the Father of life. YHWH-Elohim desires to represent himself on earth through us, and to fellowship with us. YHWH-Elohim defines the parameters for life and work. He permits Satan to test commitment and relationship.

3. EL ELYON: Abram and Melchizedek, Genesis 14

The Most High God, eternal King who rules over all is the owner of the universe, creator and possessor of heaven and earth. He is CEO and administrator of all of life, high priest worthy of our tithes, and Deliverer of our enemies into our hands. He is the One who delivers us from destruction.

4. ADONAI: Abram and the Promise of an Heir, Genesis 15

Shield, Great Reward, and Sovereign God is the One who justifies sinners through making covenant. He protects his own. Adonai is Master and Redeemer, Lord of destinies and inheritance. He guarantees his promises with his own life. He is promise maker and promise keeper.

5. EL SHADDAI: Abraham's New Name and Circumcision, Genesis 17

God Almighty with invincible power and provision and enormous abundance is the multi-generational God who confirms the everlasting covenant, circumcises our hearts, and provides inheritance. He is the covenant keeper who calls us to lay down all we hold dear in this life to be called by his name and reflect his character.

6. YHWH, the Great I AM: Moses' First Call to Holiness, Exodus 3-12

The dependable God who exists with no limits, calls us out of Egypt/our old life style, to worship YHWH, the great I Am. He is the God who desires our relationship and love and worship. He is holy and has absolute and final authority over all that exists.

7. YHWH, the LORD: Moses Call to God's Presence, Exodus 34:5-7

The Lord, the Lord is the compassionate and gracious One, whose glory is goodness and whose power changes us and fulfills his purposes. He is slow to anger, patient and longsuffering, abounding in covenant love, faithfulness, and loyalty. He maintains love to thousands, forgives lawlessness, rebellion, and sin; he is just, and holds sin accountable.

8. QADOSH: Isaiah, Isaiah 6-7, 42, 53

Holy God is the Lord who separates us to himself. HE is HOLY. Holiness is YHWH'S essence and refers to his character, the inner essence of his person. He is Immanuel, God with us, Wonderful Counselor, Mighty God, Everlasting Father, Prince of Peace.

9. QABOD: Ezekiel: Ezekiel 1, 9-11

Glorious, the Lord who is majestic, brilliant, heavy, weighty, important, and honored, who shares his Glory, and very presence with his people. YHWH is the *qabod* of the righteous: his power, authority and honor. Glory is the outer garment of holiness that people can see. Jesus is the

10. FATHER IN HEAVEN/ BELOVED SON, JESUS in the Book of John

"Our Father in Heaven, holy is your name.... to whom belongs the kingdom, power and glory." Father said of Jesus: "This is my beloved Son whom I love. With him I AM well pleased." He's my "One and Only Son." Jesus said of himself and Father: "Before Abraham lived, I AM." "I and the Father are one." "I AM the way, the truth and the life. No one comes to the Father except through me."

11. THE GOD AND FATHER OF OUR LORD JESUS CHRIST: Acts and Writings of the Apostles

The God and Father of our Lord Jesus Christ is the Glorious Father, from whom his whole family in heaven and on earth derives its name. He is the One who gives the Word of God, the glorious God, the God of all grace, the God who gives endurance, encouragement and compassion. He is the God of all comfort.

12. HOLY SPIRIT: Jesus, John 14-17

Worship YHWH through Jesus in the Holy Spirit. Jesus calls the Holy Spirit the Spirit of Truth, the Counselor, the Teacher, the One Who Testifies about Jesus, and the One Who Convicts.

13. One-Who-Sits-On–The-Throne: John, Revelation 4

The One-who-sits-on–the-throne and who lives forever and ever is the Lord God Almighty, who was and is and is to come, the Authority, the Eternal One, the Worthy One, the Creator.

14. THE LION-LAMB: John, Revelation 5-22

Lion-Lamb, Lamb Who Was Slain is the Uncreated Lion who springs from the tribe of Judah, the Root of David. Only he is Worthy to open the scroll. He is King of kings and Lord of lords, Alpha and Omega, the Worthy One... and so many more self-revealed names yet to be revealed, worthy only of YHWH.

YHWH in David's Psalms

It is King David who bears the part of YHWH's progressive revelation that always looks forward to the coming of Father's One and Only, Jesus, the Messiah-King. Close as he was to the heart of YHWH, we have no record of specific encounters associated with self-revealed names. Instead, we have a flow of revelation in the Psalms that declare new names that David used to worship YHWH.

In the Psalms, New Testament believers today are shown how to worship the Lord constantly from the heart with thanksgiving, praise, and petition, as David and his priests worshipped in Jerusalem for 40 years. King David's consistent and open approach to YHWH's presence yielded for us the wealth of psalms that constitute David's bequest to the New Testament Church. You can picture David bowing before the Divine Glory, reveling in his proximity to YHWH and receiving the gracious ministrations of God's presence into David's life and thinking. We too can fall before his Presence and experience the nearness of YHWH.

David became King over all Israel about 1000 B.C. All the tribes swore allegiance to him by accepting Samuel's prophetic word of anointing on David (2 Samuel 5:1-5). With his army, David acted as both general and government leader, captured Jerusalem from the Jebusites and transformed this insignificant provincial capital into his royal residence and kingly city and place of worship for YHWH, his Living God.

Encountering the Context for Davidic Worship

In order to comprehend David's Psalms, it is necessary to understand their historic context. Before David came on the scene, the

Philistines had defeated Israel in war and captured the Ark of the LORD (I Samuel 4:11-12). But because of the presence of the Ark they suffered inexplicable plagues and death. With such damage, they wanted the Ark out of their territory. The residents notified the citizens of Judah to come get the Ark and it finally came to rest at the house of Abinadab in Kiriath Jearim (I Samuel 7:2). There it remained some twenty years until David and his mighty men came to reclaim their inheritance. This means that for some 20 years, although sacrifices continued in the Tabernacle at Mount Gibeon, the Ark of the Covenant, the actual presence of YHWH on earth, stayed in relative obscurity.

Then David made a hasty and ill-advised attempt to move the Ark of the Covenant into Jerusalem, resulting in the death of Uzzah who was not a priest yet tried to keep the Ark from falling over. David recognized the error of his impulsive act, and appointed some priests who had YHWH's authorization to carry the Ark. Some 30,000 of David's troops returned to Abinadab's home to reclaim the Ark as Israel's identity and inheritance. With the shout of worship and sound of trumpets, David with his men danced the whole distance before the Lord into Jerusalem. What an amazing dance before the Lord that must have been!

THE DAVIDIC TABERNACLE IN JERUSALEM. For 20 years there were two centers for YHWH worship. The Ark of the Covenant had been brought to Jerusalem (I Chronicles 16:1), but the Tabernacle was still 20 miles northeast in Mt. Gibeon. David and the Levitical priests set up worship in a tent structure in Jerusalem that housed the Ark of the Covenant. Here they ministered with music (I Chronicles 16:4-6). Notice that the writer of Chronicles calls the Tent of Meeting the Tabernacle with Abiathar as lead priest. And yet, the original Tabernacle and Tent of Meeting had also been left functioning at the high place in Gibeon. There, David had left priests with their leader-priest Zadok to present burnt offerings to the LORD in accordance with the Law of Moses (I Chronicles 16:39-42).

So in effect, two Tabernacles were functioning at the same time: the original one at the high place in Gibeon and the other one for which David had pitched a tent in Jerusalem. In the royal city, they presented burnt offerings and fellowship offerings just once, to inaugurate the Tent. For the next forty years, the priests in Jerusalem ministered before the Lord, before the Ark of the Covenant and the Presence between the cherubim, making petition, giving thanks and praising the LORD (YHWH), the God (Elohim) of Israel.

THE MEANING OF THE DAVIDIC TABERNACLE FOR BELIEVERS TODAY. In the Acts of the Apostles there is another expression of this Davidic Tabernacle, one that has meaning for the New Testament believer. Luke set it in the context of the early Church's struggle to include Gentile converts within the Church of Jesus Christ. At the Jerusalem Council in Acts 15, Barnabas and Paul shared about the Lord's work in Gentile provinces and the establishment of churches. Then, Peter presented his personal experiences among Gentiles upon whom the Holy Spirit had fallen and bestowed his gifts.

James, the brother of our Lord and leader of the Council, concluded the discussion on the relationship of the church to the Gentiles by quoting Amos 9:11-12. Amos said that YHWH was to return and rebuild David's fallen tent, rebuilding its ruins and restoring it so that the remnant of men and all Gentiles might seek the Lord (Acts 15:16-17) "After this I will return and rebuild David's fallen tent. Its ruins I will rebuild, and I will restore it, that the remnant of men may seek the Lord, and all the Gentiles who bear my name, says the Lord, who does these things that have been known for ages." James equates the entrance of Gentiles into Christ's Church with the restoration of David's fallen tent.

The Apostolic Council then released Gentile converts from obedience to the Mosaic Law. The connection can be found in the above passages when God had released David and the priests from the Mosaic ordinances concerning the Ark of the Covenant—thus allowing direct and open approach to YHWH's very presence over the Ark. The priests, with David, then practiced worship by thanksgiving, praise and petition for about 40 years in Jerusalem. In the same way, according to these New Testament apostles, God had released Gentile converts from obedience to the Mosaic Law—thus allowing direct and open approach to YHWH's presence through the Holy Spirit who indwells all believers.

YHWH's Names in David's Psalms

Many of us have wondered just how it was possible for David to experience the Lord much like we experience the Lord today. Of course, David was considered a prophet and God was pleased to speak his own word directly through him. But consider David's situation: whenever he wished, he could enter the tent he had pitched for the Ark of the Covenant and fall down before YHWH's presence, between the cherubim and over the Ark. Here David experienced the nearness to YHWH that he so eloquently expressed in the Psalms.

> **David would touch such a presence of God in the temple that the people would have to leave**

Whenever David entered the temple he experienced the palpable presence of God and this was his habit of life. He declared his one desire in Psalm 27, "that I may dwell in the house of the Lord all the days of my life, to gaze upon the beauty of the Lord and to seek him in his temple." He would touch the glory of God in these times, when the presence of the Lord became so strong that people had to leave the temple.

To understand how this can happen to you, there are two standard methods of interpreting the Psalms. The first one deals with what the psalm meant to the original readers in terms of their language and culture. The second one Jesus articulated in Luke 24:44, as he appeared to his disciples: "This is what I told you while I was still with you: everything must be fulfilled that is written about me in the Law of Moses, the Prophets and the Psalms." In the second perspective, we learn to recognize Jesus and his work in the midst of the psalm we are reading. This is the focus for our discussion below.

In order to tap into the rich stream of YHWH's grace to mankind as shown in the Psalms, we will look at five groupings of psalms that are mixed with both types of interpretations. Each group has an overriding theme that is expressed in each psalm within that group. The groupings cover only some of the psalms but, hopefully, will serve as an example to encourage readers to explore the rest of the Psalms. For the apostolic and early churches, the Psalms constituted both their prayer book and their hymnbook.

The following names for YHWH God are found in particular psalms that have been recognized in church liturgy for centuries. Here God revealed his names like the Righteous One and the Strong Tower. These types of descriptive name proliferate under the Spirit's inspiration in David's life and work. These descriptive names filled David's worship in the tent prepared for the Ark of the Covenant.

Group 1: YHWH the Lord Oversees Righteous and Evil People

In this first group, the focus is on YHWH's oversight of all nations on earth, encouraging and protecting those who heed his ways and obstructing those who ignore or reject him. This is

YHWH's providence or general love-care for all people on earth. This is exemplified in Psalms 1, 2, and 11.

In Psalm 1, the "man" of verse 1 is the Lord Jesus, the model for every believer in attitude, work and lifestyle. The "wicked" epitomizes Satan's reign and work. In Psalm 2, we see Jesus Christ as sovereign and King who has already received earth's nations as his own inheritance. In Psalm 11, YHWH Jesus is upright and righteous. He actively and constantly withstands those who hate him, his people and his kingly activities on earth. Take your refuge in him!

NAME IN PSALM 1: YHWH. In this psalm, the LORD blesses the righteous, not the wicked.

To the original readers, the psalmist explained the ways that YHWH relates to both righteous and evil people.

With the focus on the person and work of Jesus Christ in this psalm, the "man" of verse 1 is the Lord Jesus, the model for every believer in attitude, work and lifestyle. The "wicked" epitomizes Satan's reign and work.

NAMES IN PSALM 2: YHWH, ANOINTED (MESSIAH), KING SON. In this psalm, YHWH deals with the unrighteous through his righteous Son, the King.

To the original readers, the psalmist showed the futility of Gentile nations as they strived to organize themselves against YHWH's sovereign, moral universe.

With the focus on the person and work of Jesus Christ in this Psalm, kings and rulers of the earth, and the present world system attempt to throw off Father's constraints built into society. He rebukes them by establishing his Son as sovereign and King who has already received earth's nations as his own inheritance.

NAMES IN PSALM 11: YHWH, YHWH IS RIGHTEOUS. In this psalm, YHWH rules over the hearts of the just and the evil.

To the original readers, though evil men attack the godly, YHWH observed, examined and destroyed all those who attack the upright in heart.

With the focus on the person and work of Jesus Christ in this psalm, he is upright and righteous. He actively and constantly withstands those who hate him, his people and his kingly activities on earth. Take your refuge in him!

GROUP 2: YHWH THE LORD ATTACKS HIS ENEMIES

In the second group of Psalms, the warfare theme in these Psalms teaches God's people how to engage the enemy and defeat him who is Jesus' main enemy, as exemplified in Psalms 3 and 9.

In Psalm 3, YHWH Jesus battles his enemies who are the enemies of his people. He is their shield and glory. We, his people attack the enemy of our souls by calling out to Jesus for deliverance. In Psalm 9, Jesus praised his Father and boasts of his Father's aggressive action to destroy his enemies. To know his name is to trust him for deliverance.

NAMES IN PSALM 3: ELOHIM, YHWH, SHIELD (SOVEREIGN), GLORIOUS ONE. In this psalm, you will find warfare tactics for the righteous.

To the original readers, the psalmist comforted YHWH's people who experience fear of the enemy. And he shows them how to engage in warfare with the LORD's enemies.

With the focus on the person and work of Jesus Christ in this psalm, Jesus battles his enemies who are the enemies of his people;

he is their shield and glory. We, his people attack the enemy of our souls by calling out to Jesus for deliverance.

NAMES IN PSALM 9: YHWH, EL ELYON. This psalm describes the struggle with our enemies.

To the original readers, the Psalmist tied together praise for YHWH, El Elyon, O Most High, with YHWH's thorough judgment on his enemies.

With the focus on the person and work of Jesus Christ in this psalm, Jesus praised his Father and boasts of his Father's aggressive action to destroy his enemies. To know his name is to trust him.

GROUP 3: YHWH THE LORD, BEAUTIFUL, RIGHTEOUS, GOD AND KING

The Lord YHWH gives his Presence to those who seek him. In this third group of Psalms, believers learn how to approach YHWH in the morning or evening, by preparing one's heart and bowing down in adoration, as shown in Psalm 4 and 5, and Psalm 27.

In Psalm 4 YHWH Jesus is our righteousness and clears our offenses. He cries out to Father about people who offend him deeply. In this way, the believer will lie down and sleep in peace. In Psalm 5, Jesus makes his requests known to Father that he remove the arrogant, lead him in a straight path of obedience and judge the earth in righteousness. In Psalm 27, Jesus is our light, our salvation, our stronghold, the one we desire, that we may gaze on his beauty and seek him in his temple. Here the focus is on seeking and waiting on him as our heart's safe home.

NAMES IN PSALM 4: ELOHIM, TSEDEKI (MY RIGHTEOUSNESS) YHWH, EL ELYON. He clears the offenses.

To the original readers, the very human experience of anger from offenses is seen, with offering sacrifices and trusting the Lord for approval as the only Righteous One.

With the focus on the person and work of Jesus Christ in this psalm, Jesus, our sacrifice, cries to his Father about people who offend him deeply. In this way, the believer will lie down and sleep in peace.

NAMES IN PSALM 5: YHWH, ELOHIM. Seek his presence and bow down in his presence.

> **In worship our focus is on seeking, waiting on him as our heart's safe home**

To the original readers, this is a morning plea to YHWH to exclude the arrogant and receive those who bow down.

With the focus on the person and work of Jesus Christ in this psalm, Jesus makes his requests known to Father that he remove the arrogant, lead him in a straight path of obedience and judge the earth in righteousness.

GROUP 4: YHWH THE MERCIFUL GOD ENCOUNTERS HIS PEOPLE THROUGH CONTRITION, LAMENTATION AND FORGIVENESS

Many centuries ago, the Church recognized and named a list of psalms that focused the believer on the repentance cycle, an activity urgently necessary for the believer's nearness in fellowship with God and growth in the grace of God. This fourth group, called "penitential psalms," includes Psalms 6, 32, 38, 51, 102, 130 and 143.

Psalm 6 is our example here – a plea for mercy while suffering. Jesus experienced Father's awful displeasure with sin and affirms YHWH's mercy to him, and so on us.

NAME IN PSALM 6: YHWH. This psalm is a plea for mercy while suffering.

To the original readers, the afflicted pleaded to abate suffering, based on YHWH's unfailing love.

With the focus on the person and work of Jesus Christ in this psalm, Jesus experienced Father's awful displeasure with sin and affirms YHWH's mercy to him, and so on us.

GROUP 5: YHWH ELOHIM, EL ELYON, MY DELIGHT, THE HOLY ONE

This final group of Psalms interpret Jesus' daily experiences as the God-man on earth, as he fulfilled Father's purposes, as seen in Psalms 7 and 16.

In Psalm 7, Jesus suffered redemptively on the Day of Atonement. This is a psalm of the Lord's redemptive sufferings at the hands of injustice, describing Jesus' pathway to Calvary and his death. In Psalm 16, Jesus' death and resurrection is the path to our life and inheritance. Jesus rejoiced in his comrades, the inheritance Father assigned to him, and his deliverance from death.

As you read these Psalms, take note of other names of God shared: My King, The Holy One, Seed of David, The Lord Strong and Mighty, the Lord Strong in Battle, the Lord of Hosts, the Righteous One, Servant, Priest Forever, Shepherd of Israel, the Headstone of the Corner, Lord our Maker, Habitation, Defense, Shield, Rock, and others.

NAMES IN PSALM 7: YHWH, ELOHIM, EL ELYON. Jesus suffered redemptively on the Day of Atonement.

To the original readers, a penitent wrestles to understand his sin and calls on God to vindicate him from his enemies.

With the focus on the person and work of Jesus Christ, this is a psalm of the Lord's redemptive sufferings at the hands of injustice, describing Jesus' pathway to Calvary and his death.

NAMES IN PSALM 16: ELOHIM, YHWH, MY DELIGHT, HOLY ONE. Jesus' death and resurrection is the path to our life and inheritance.

To the original readers, the focus was on a believer's affirmation of confidence in Father's power to sustain him in life and death.

With the focus on the person and work of Jesus Christ in this psalm, Jesus rejoiced in his comrades, the inheritance Father assigned to him, and his deliverance from death.

As you read all the Psalms, take note of these and other names of God shared in each psalm: My King, The Holy One, Seed of David, The Lord Strong and Mighty, the Lord Strong in Battle, the Lord of Hosts, the Righteous One, Servant, Priest Forever, Shepherd of Israel, the Headstone of the Corner, Lord our Maker, Habitation, Defense, Shield, Rock, and others.

NAMES IN PSALM 16: ELOHIM, YHWH, MY DELIGHT, HOLY ONE. Jesus' death and resurrection is the path to our life and inheritance.

To the original readers, the focus was on a believer's affirmation of confidence in Father's power to sustain him in life and death.

With the focus on the person and work of Jesus Christ in this psalm, Jesus rejoiced in his comrades, the inheritance Father assigned to him, and his deliverance from death.

> **He will draw you into quietness where you can savor his presence and experience his Word to you**

A patient reading of each psalm will show you the perceptive gift on David for recognizing God's intrusive activities in life and hearing and naming him accordingly. Recognize David's way of describing God, so that you can worship God through his names, names he will give you too.

WORSHIPING YHWH WITH DAVID

The greatest accolade the Lord gave to David was that he was, "a man after my own heart." David worked for years to bring himself into line with YHWH Elohim, the One who is Good, Holy, and Glorious. David's Psalms overflow with this perspective: "I want to be like God in heart and attitude." Let David's Psalms help you express how you feel about and relate with the Living God.

THANK YHWH. As you list off the innumerable names and acts of God in your behalf, the LORD will begin to open the door into his presence. By faith, know that he is opening the door for you to enter. You already know how much he wants you to come. Offer thanks to God at every point you can.

PRAISE YHWH. Use these psalms before the LORD as a way of showering him with praise. With your list of names from this chapter or from your own readings, begin to thank and praise him that he is the person these names indicate. Let your love for him flow to him.

WORSHIP YHWH. This is the transition time. As you have been expressing to God your thanksgiving and praise, now affirm in your own mind his goodness to you. Start to expect his presence to filter into you more and more. Spend time alternating between active thanks-praise and quietness before him. He will draw you into quietness so that you can begin to savor his presence and experience his Word to you: not merely words heard by ear, but more important the Word who is the presence of God. His presence goes far beyond human speech. His presence comes to wash and erase, to cleanse and purge, to infuse and fill, to impart and permeate with his Spirit.

ADORE YHWH. In this quiet time, a time of silence by yourself in the presence of our God, let his presence flow over and around you. Wait for the LORD, wait I say, for the LORD. Out of the unfathomable depths of his presence and person, he will form within you an awareness of himself, sometimes an image of himself, sometimes a series of words or parables about himself. Wait on the LORD. He is coming! He is here!

GROUP 1: THE LORD-YHWH OVERSEES RIGHTEOUS AND EVIL PEOPLE

In this first group, the focus is on YHWH's oversight of all nations on earth, encouraging and protecting those who heed his ways and obstructing those who ignore or reject him. This is YHWH's providence or general love-care for all people on earth. This is exemplified in Psalms 1, 2, and 11.

NAME IN PSALM 1: YHWH. In this psalm, the LORD blesses the righteous, not the wicked.

To the original readers, the psalmist explained the ways that YHWH relates to both righteous and evil people.

With the focus on the person and work of Jesus Christ in this psalm, the "man" of verse 1 is the Lord Jesus, the model for every believer in attitude, work and lifestyle. The "wicked" epitomizes Satan's reign and work.

NAMES IN PSALM 2: YHWH, ANOINTED (MESSIAH), KING SON. In this psalm, YHWH deals with the unrighteous through his righteous Son, the King.

To the original readers, the psalmist showed the futility of Gentile nations as they strived to organize themselves against YHWH's sovereign, moral universe.

With the focus on the person and work of Jesus Christ in this Psalm, kings and rulers of the earth, and the present world system attempt to throw off Father's constraints built into society. He rebukes them by establishing his Son as sovereign and King who has already received earth's nations as his own inheritance.

NAMES IN PSALM 11: YHWH, YHWH IS RIGHTEOUS. In this psalm, YHWH rules over the hearts of the just and the evil.

To the original readers, though evil men attack the godly, YHWH observed, examined and destroyed all those who attack the upright in heart.

With the focus on the person and work of Jesus Christ in this psalm, he is upright and righteous. He actively and constantly withstands those who hate him, his people and his kingly activities on earth. Take your refuge in him!

GROUP 2: THE LORD-YHWH ATTACKS HIS ENEMIES THROUGH HIS PEOPLE

In the second group of Psalms, the warfare theme in these Psalms teaches God's people how to engage the enemy and defeat him who is Jesus' main enemy, as exemplified in Psalms 3 and 9.

NAMES IN PSALM 3: ELOHIM, YHWH, SHIELD (SOVEREIGN), GLORIOUS ONE. In this psalm, you will find warfare tactics for the righteous.

To the original readers, the psalmist comforted YHWH's people who experience fear of the enemy. And he shows them how to engage in warfare with the LORD's enemies.

With the focus on the person and work of Jesus Christ in this psalm, Jesus battles his enemies who are the enemies of his people; he is their shield and glory. We, his people attack the enemy of our souls by calling out to Jesus for deliverance.

NAMES IN PSALM 9: YHWH, EL ELYON. This psalm describes the struggle with our enemies.

To the original readers, the Psalmist tied together praise for YHWH, El Elyon, O Most High, with YHWH's thorough judgment on his enemies.

With the focus on the person and work of Jesus Christ in this psalm, Jesus praised his Father and boasts of his Father's aggressive action to destroy his enemies. To know his name is to trust him.

GROUP 3: THE BELIEVER SEEKS THE LORD'S PRESENCE

The third group of Psalms shows believers how to approach YHWH in the morning or evening, by preparing one's heart and bowing down in adoration, as shown in Psalm 4 and 5, and other Psalms such as Psalm 27.

NAMES IN PSALM 4: ELOHIM, TSEDEKI (MY RIGHTEOUSNESS) YHWH, EL ELYON. He clears the offenses.

To the original readers, the very human experience of anger from offenses is seen, with offering sacrifices and trusting the Lord for approval as the only Righteous One.

With the focus on the person and work of Jesus Christ in this psalm, Jesus, our sacrifice, cries to his Father about people who offend him deeply. In this way, the believer will lie down and sleep in peace.

NAMES IN PSALM 5: YHWH, ELOHIM. Seek his presence and bow down in his presence.

To the original readers, this is a morning plea to YHWH to exclude the arrogant and receive those who bow down.

With the focus on the person and work of Jesus Christ in this psalm, Jesus makes his requests known to Father that he remove the arrogant, lead him in a straight path of obedience and judge the earth in righteousness.

GROUP 4: ENCOUNTERING YHWH THROUGH CONTRITION, LAMENTATION AND FORGIVENESS

Many centuries ago, the Church recognized and named a list of psalms that focused the believer on the repentance cycle, an activity urgently necessary for the believer's nearness in fellowship with God and growth in the grace of God. This fourth group, called "penitential psalms," includes Psalms 6, 32, 38, 51, 102, 130 and 143. Let these psalms guide you in how to maintain a repentant attitude, and when and how to exercise that attitude before YHWH. Psalm 6 is our example here.

NAME IN PSALM 6: YHWH. This psalm is a plea for mercy while suffering.

To the original readers, the afflicted pleaded to abate suffering, based on YHWH's unfailing love.

With the focus on the person and work of Jesus Christ in this psalm, Jesus experienced Father's awful displeasure with sin and affirms YHWH's mercy to him, and so on us.

GROUP 5: ENCOUNTERING YHWH THROUGH DAVID'S REVELATION OF JESUS' EXPERIENCES

These psalms interpret Jesus' daily experiences as the God-man on earth, as he fulfilled Father's purposes. Here are some samples.

NAMES IN PSALM 7: YHWH, ELOHIM, EL ELYON. Jesus suffered redemptively on the Day of Atonement.

To the original readers, a penitent wrestles to understand his sin and calls on God to vindicate him from his enemies.

With the focus on the person and work of Jesus Christ, this is a psalm of the Lord's redemptive sufferings at the hands of injustice, describing Jesus' pathway to Calvary and his death.

NAMES IN PSALM 16: ELOHIM, YHWH, MY DELIGHT, HOLY ONE. Jesus' death and resurrection is the path to our life and inheritance.

To the original readers, the focus was on a believer's affirmation of confidence in Father's power to sustain him in life and death.

With the focus on the person and work of Jesus Christ in this psalm, Jesus rejoiced in his comrades, the inheritance Father assigned to him, and his deliverance from death.

As you read all the Psalms, take note of these and other names of God shared in each psalm: My King, The Holy One, Seed of David, The Lord Strong and Mighty, the Lord Strong in Battle, the Lord of Hosts, the Righteous One, Servant, Priest Forever, Shepherd of Israel, the Headstone of the Corner, Lord our Maker, Habitation, Defense, Shield, Rock, and others.

A patient reading of each psalm will show you the perceptive gift on David for recognizing God's intrusive activities in life and hearing and naming him accordingly. Recognize David's way of describing God, so that you can worship God through his Names, Names he will give you too.

Worship Words
With Numbers from Strong's Concordance

1245 BAQASH (BAW-KASH'). To seek, to search out, to set about.

1875 DARASH (DAW-RASH'). To resort to, to seek or ask, to search, to inquire.

3034 YADAH (YAW-DAW') plus 3027 YAD (YAWD) To confess, to use the hand, to throw, to give praise, to give thanks with hands, to revere or worship using hands.

5066 NAGASH (NAW-GASH'). To draw near, to approach, to bring.

5456 SAGAD (SAW-GAD'). To bow down, to fall down, to prostrate oneself (in worship).

5457 SEGID (SEG-EED). To do homage, to worship.

5647 ABAD (AW-BAD'). To work, to serve as slaves.

6279 ATHAR (AW-THAR'). To pray, to supplicate, to entreat.

6282 ATHAR (AW-THAWR'). A worshiper, often using incense.

6399 PELACH (PEL-AKH'). To serve, to pay reverence to.

6402 POLCHAN (POL-KHAWN') Worship, service.

6999 QATAR (KAW-TAR'). To make sacrifices, to smoke, to make fragrance by fire, to burn incense.

7812 SHACHAH (SHAW-KHAW'). To bow down, to make oneself prostrate, to pay homage to God.

8334 SHARATH (SHAW-RATH'). To attend, to minister, to serve, to wait on.

8426 TODAH (TO-DAW) Thanksgiving and praise.

Recommendations for Further Study

Many of these books are available used at on-line sources such ABE Books and Amazon.

YHWH-Elohim

John D Currid (1997). *Ancient Egypt and the Old Testament.* Baker Books, Grand Rapids.

Carl F Henry (1948). *Notes on the Doctrine of God.* W. A. Wilde Co; Chicago. Especially note the chapter on "The Names of God."

Johs Pedersen (1973). *Israel, Its Life and Culture,* Vol. 1-4. Oxford University Press, London. Especially note Vol. I-II, p. 245 about the "Name."

Covenant in the Hittite Culture

The Hittite culture made extensive use of a covenant system unlike anything known today in our Western world. For more information about common Mesopotamian legal practices for that area and era, see the following sources:

D.N. Freedman, editor (2000). *Eerdmans Dictionary of the Bible.* Grand Rapids: Eerdmans.

A Millard and D. Wiseman, editors (1983). *Essays on the Patriarchal Narratives.* Winona Lake.

John Trane (1987). *Introducing the Old Testament.* Herts, England: Lion Book. Especially note pages 44-45.

Gleason Archer, Jr (1974). *A Survey of Old Testament Introduction.* Chicago: Moody Press. Especially note the Nuzi Tablets, pages 116, 137, 170-71, 266

EL ELYON

Diane Wolkstein & Samuel Noah Kramer (1983). *Inanna (Queen of Heaven and Earth, Her Stories and Hymns from Sumer).* NY: Harper Row Publishers.

Janathan N. Tubb. (1998). *Canaanities, People of the Past.* Norman, OK: Univ. of Oklahoma Press.

YHWH AS MOSES ENCOUNTERED HIM:

Alan Cole (1973). *Exodus, Introduction and Commentary.* Tyndale.

Alan Cole (1973). *Old Testament Commentaries.* Inter Varsity Press.

John D. Currid (1999). *Ancient Egypt and the Old Testament.* Baker Book House.

John J. Davis (1979). *Moses and the Gods of Egypt (Studies in Exodus).* Baker Book House.

Frank E. Gabelein (1990), General Editor: *The Expositor's Bible Commentary, with N.I.V.* Zondervan.

Henry H. Halley (1965). *Halley's Bible Handbook.* Zondervan.

Nahum M. Sarna (1980). *Exploring Exodus (The Heritage of Biblical Israel).* Schoken Books, New York.

RECOMMENDATIONS FOR FURTHER STUDY

GLORY: 'QABOD' AND HOLY: 'KADOSH'

G. Johannes Botterweck, Helmer Ringgren, Heinz-Josef Fabry (1995). *Theological Dictionary of the Old Testament*, Grand Rapids: Eerdmans

Colin Brown, editor (1997). *The New international Dictionary of New Testament Theology*, Vol. 2. Grand Rapids: Zondervan

Robert Baker Girdlestone (1951). *Synonyms of the Old Testament (Their Bearing on Christian Doctrine)*. Grand Rapids: Eerdmans. Especially note chapter XV, "Sanctify, Sacred, Holy."

R. Laird Harris, Gleason L. Archer, Jr., Bruce K. Waltke (1980). *Theological Wordbook of the Old Testament*. Chicago: Moody Press.

William L. Holladay, Editor (1988). *A Concise Hebrew and Aramaic Lexicon of the Old Testament*. Grand Rapids: Eerdmans.

Barri Cae Mallin & Shmuel Wolkenfeld (1999). *Intimate Moments with the Hebrew Names of God*. Bridge-Logos Publishers. Recommended for your devotional life.

Aaron Pick (1977). *Dictionary of Old Testament Words for English Readers*. Kregel Publications.

W. E. Vine, edited by F. F. Bruce (1978). *An Expository Dictionary of Old Testament Words*. New York: Revell Co.

THE APOSTLES' WORSHIP

Allen Cabaniss (1989). *Pattern in Early Christian Worship.* Mercer University Press, Macon, GA.

Judson Cornwall (1996). *Worship as David Lived It.* Revival Press, Destiny Image.

Oscar Cullmann (1953). *Early Christian Worship.* Wyndham Hall Press.

Joseph Garlington (1998). *Worship (The Pattern of Things in Heaven).* Destiny Image.

Daniel Liderbach (1998). *Christ in the Early Christian Hymns.* Paulist Press

Herbert Lockyer (1990). *All the Prayers of the Bible.* Zondervan.

Robert E. Webber, editor (1994), *The Complete Library of Christian Worship, Vol. 2: Twenty Centuries of Christian Worship.* StarSong Publishers.

Robert E. Webber (1999). *Ancient-Future Faith, A Brief History of Christian Worship.* Grand Rapids, MI: Baker Books.

James F. White (1999). *A Brief History of Christian Worship.* Nashville, TN: Abingdon Press.

1st and 2nd Century works: *The Didache. Ignatius of Antioch on the Epistle to the Ephesians and Epistle to the Magnesians,* by Justin, 1st and 2nd century apologist for the Christian faith, and Clement of Rome, on the Epistle to the Corinthians.

Made in the USA
Coppell, TX
07 February 2021